B+T 10/00

D0851871

A LONG HAUL

B+T 10/00

A LONG HAUL

The Story of the
New York State Barge Canal

3 1571 00192 8277

MICHELE A. McFEE

GLEN COVE PUBLIC LIBRARY
4 GLEN COVE AVENUE
GLEN COVE, NEW YORK 11542-2885

PURPLE MOUNTAIN PRESS ◆ FLEISCHMANNS, NEW YORK

Published by
Purple Mountain Press, Ltd.
Main Street, P.O. Box E3
Fleischmanns, New York 12430-0378
(914) 254-4062
Fax (914) 254-4476

Copyright © 1998 by Michele A. McFee

First Edition

All rights reserved under International and Pan-American Copyright Conventions.
No part of this book may be reproduced or transmitted in any form without
permission in writing from the publisher and copyright holder.

Library of Congress Cataloging-in-Publication Data

McFee, Michele A. (Michele Ann), 1961-
    A long haul : the story of the New York State Barge Canal / Michele A. McFee.
        p.   cm.
    Includes bibliographical references and index.
    ISBN 0-935796-99-1 (pbk. : alk. paper)
    1. New York State Barge Canal System (N.Y.) — History. 2. Canals — New York (State) — History. I. Title.
HE395.N77M38 1998
386'.48'09747 — dc21
                                         98-26211
                                         CIP

ISBN 0-935796-99-1

Book design and typesetting by Jerry Novesky

Manufactured in the United States of America
Printed on acid-free paper

9 8 7 6 5 4 3 2 1

Frontis: A steam tugboat with its tow of barges emerging from the lower end of Lock
17 at Little Falls, 1921.   *New York State Archives*

To my son Andy, who needs to know how everything works

Contents

Help for the Long Haul

I could not have written a book that brings out so many facets of a great public work spanning so many years over such a large geographic area without the input of many people, all of whom have made special contributions.

Many individuals allowed me a special glimpse into their lives that helped me bring out the complete story of the canal. They include Chuck Dwyer, Fred Godfrey, Dan Geist, Dennis Fishette, Ralph Folger, Bill Hills, Joseph Mosso, Bill and Sue Orzell, Joe Stellato, Dan Wiles, and Evamay Wilkins.

Individuals in the New York State Canal Corporation, a subsidiary of the New York State Thruway Authority, were also very helpful in explaining how the canal operates and making resource material available to me. It was a pleasure to work specifically with Bill Clifford, Joe Donovan, Keith Giles, John Jermano, Larry O'Connor, Mike Monahan, Bill Pittsley, Fred Sokolowski, and the crews of the state tugs who let me tag along and get underfoot. The crew of the *Ward's Island* was especially gracious to let me come along on a cold December day on the Oneida River and to tell me their stories. Thanks also to the many lock operators and other canal employees for sharing their enthusiasm and pride in the Barge Canal with me. The Canal Corporation also made it possible for me to ride along on a number of Barge Canal inspection tours in 1994 and 1995, which allowed me the freedom to explore the different parts of the canal.

I want to thank the Canal Society of New York State for making its Barge Canal material available to me; more specifically, I'd like to thank the members of the society who encouraged me by their sustained interest in the book. I also appreciate the society's effort in putting together two well-researched field trips each year to canals in different parts of the state. The field trips, accompanying guidebooks, and stimulating discussions and debates made me aware of little-known aspects of the canal.

I also was influenced by the books of Fred G. Godfrey, Richard Garrity, and Charles T. O'Malley, whose previous writings captured the spirit of the Barge Canal.

Thanks also to the New York State Archives and the New York State Museum for letting me use their Barge Canal collections; to Lynn McCarthy at New York State Electric and Gas for locating pictures of power plants; to Linda DeVona for her striking drawing of the lighthouse.

Thanks to those who read the manuscript for historical accuracy: Joe Stellato, retired head of operations for the New York State Barge Canal; Fred Godfrey, retired tugboat captain; and Tom Grasso, president of the Canal Society of New York State and chair of the geology department at Monroe Community College. A special thanks goes to Dan Mordell, a founding member of the Canal Society of New York State, who showed his support for my project by trusting me with his personal collection of Barge Canal materials. I also appreciate the patience and encouragement of my publishers, Wray and Loni Rominger, who had an even greater vision for the project than I did.

I am thankful for the sustained enthusiasm my family showed for the project. My children—Sarah, Andy, and Christopher—came along eagerly on countless canal explorations until the project got into their blood, too. My husband Ed showed a spirit of adventure and continuous support and interest in the book that made it an enjoyable topic to tackle.

I will always be indebted to Craig Williams, curator, New York State Museum. His hand in making this book happen should never be underestimated.

Even with such assistance, I take full responsibility for any factual errors or misinterpretations that might appear in the text.

Foreword

The Erie Canal was the most successful nineteenth-century undertaking of its kind in the United States. Although several eastern states such as Pennsylvania, Maryland, and Virginia constructed canals that attempted to unite the interior of the country with the eastern seaboard, none would prove as beneficial as the Erie Canal. Of all the eastern canals, it is the only one still in operation—boats can still pass from Buffalo to Albany on the Erie Canal, although on a slightly altered course from its nineteenth-century location. The success of the Erie canal is in turn rooted in the underlying geology, lay of the land, and stream patterns.

The ink on the early landscape maps of northeast North America had barely dried when it became readily apparent that nature had bequeathed to New York a rich and remarkable inheritance. Christopher Colles remarked on this astoundingly dramatic topographic effect in 1784 when he wrote that the "Allegheny mountains . . . seem to die away as they approach the Mohawk River . . ." This fortuitous stroke of geological luck gives New York State an enormous advantage over other eastern states: There are no major highlands between the Hudson River at Albany and Lake Erie. There is the additional, splendid, blessing of New York's river and stream drainage pattern along and north of the Albany–Buffalo parallel. *The rivers and streams flow either east or west!* This drainage pattern is made even more significant by one more salient feature—it lies below the level of Lake Erie. If only Lake Erie water could be channeled eastward, the natural drainage and lay of the land could be utilized for much of the remaining distance to the Hudson River. Lake Erie water filled the Erie Canal as far as the Seneca River.

From Palmyra to the Hudson River, belts of shale, easily weakened by weathering and erosion, eventually formed valleys that could be used as a corridor for the Erie Canal with relative ease and little expense. Pennsylvania, on the other hand, had intervening high mountains and a lack of properly aligned streams, which posed awesome obstacles in its attempt to unite Philadelphia with Pittsburgh by canal.

Even with all of its natural advantages, New York State's canal effort was not without its difficulties. Several daunting obstacles had to be overcome. They are, from east to west: the "Great Falls" of the Mohawk at Cohoes and the bedrock gorge of the lower Mohawk River just east of Schenectady to the Hudson River; the falls and rapids at Little Falls; the Montezuma marshes; the crossing of the deep Irondequoit Valley between Fairport and Pittsford; and the Niagara Escarpment at Lockport.

The present Erie Canal division of the Barge Canal System is the fourth iteration of the Erie Canal. Clinton's Ditch, the original canal, was 40 feet wide at water surface and 4 feet deep, yet it could float boats with a maximum cargo capacity of 70 tons. Transportation costs by canal across the state were lowered more than 90 percent. The original Erie was so choked with craft that in only ten years, from the tolls generated, it not only showed a profit but contributed substantially to the general state budget, thereby significantly offsetting the cost of government. This enormous success prompted the first enlargement of the Erie.

The Enlarged Erie was the second Erie Canal, and its sporadic construction, mostly on line with Clinton's Ditch, spanned the years 1835 to 1862. A new artificial channel was constructed across the state—70 feet wide at water surface and 7 feet deep—capable of floating 240 tons per boat and reducing shipping costs an additional 50 percent. In general, locks were rebuilt and relocated with larger dimensions, and with a second chamber added alongside the first to permit the locking of two boats simultaneously. Aqueducts also were relocated and enlarged.

By the 1890s the railroads had diverted some of the trade from the canal, leaving the Erie with a shrinking percentage of transported goods, although its annual tonnage did not drop significantly. Canal engineers believed another enlargement was the key to countering this competition, as boats carrying higher tonnages would be more efficient, thereby further reducing transportation costs. The Nine–Million–Dollar Improvement of 1895 was the third Erie Canal. Its primary objective was to deepen the channel from 7 feet to 9 feet. By 1898 the $9 million had been expended, but the new channel was far from complete. Amid a storm of controversy involving charges of fraud and incompetence, a stop law was enacted in 1898 which brought the much-maligned project to an immediate and perhaps grateful end.

The following year, Governor Theodore Roosevelt embarked on a thorough study of New York's canal system when he appointed the Committee on Canals to accomplish the task. The "Report of the Committee on Canals," issued in 1900, was a revolutionary document that formed the bedrock for further studies and surveys, culminating in construction of the Barge Canal System, completed in 1918.

The canal is an outgrowth of and an intricate part of the natural landscape of New York State. It represents an intertwining of natural and human history. Geologic events in the dim past resulted in a landscape that was destined for greatness and success. It was almost as though nature was dictating that a canal would one day go across New York State and humans were only humbly following nature's dictum.

Michele McFee has written an historically accurate, fascinating, and well-researched account of the New York State Barge Canal System—especially the Erie. The reader will become immediately engrossed by her lively style of writing and how well she illuminates the canal's day-to-day operation of locks, dams, and reservoirs that regulate the flow of water. Furthermore, interests will be piqued by sections dealing with daily life on the canal, shippers, tugboat captains and operators, and commodities that once were commonplace on the canal. You will be drawn into this work as inexorably as the upstream current created when filling a lock. And you will find yourself wanting more, waiting with anticipation for what's "around the next bend," as though you were a barge canal captain piloting for the first time your own vessel and tow. It's smooth sailing ahead.

—*Thomas X. Grasso, President, Canal Society of New York State*

Introduction

The New York State Barge Canal System has struggled with an identity crisis its whole life. Not all New Yorkers wanted it. Once built, there was talk of giving it away. Now, people are not sure why it still exists. It is so long that few have had the opportunity to appreciate all its wonderful sites. It has been around so long that few can remember what is important about it.

The Barge Canal is the 1918 improvement to the New York canal system designed to allow for 3,000-ton barges—nearly a tenfold increase over what had been a normal load before it was built. Despite the lack of interest of many New Yorkers, the improvement came from what an observer at the time called "the insistent and persistent cry for cheaper rates, quicker time and increased facilities for that tide of traffic."[1] This cry for enlargement had been heard throughout the life of the very successful Erie Canal and had already led to several improvements—first resulting in the Enlarged Erie Canal, which nearly doubled its 1825 "Clinton's Ditch" dimensions. At the turn of the century, though, demand came for an even more dramatic change.

When New York Governor Theodore Roosevelt appointed a committee in 1899 to study the state's canals, he marked a clear line between the old and new attitudes New York State had toward its canals. The Barge Canal is as much a "modernization" of the original canal as it was an "enlargement." Progressive engineering and construction methods allowed it to succeed well into the twentieth century where the old canal would have come up lacking. Many New Yorkers enthusiastically embraced the new canal when they learned the state was willing to scrap the technology of the nineteenth-century Erie Canal, with its old-fashioned animal-powered boats and hand-operated locks, and was instead committed to a "modern" waterway. A visiting engineer, amazed that the people of New York State had undertaken such a project, respected their decision to complete a task that even an entire nation would think twice about taking on.[2]

The enterprise was an evolutionary step in thought as well as engineering. Building it was only part of the battle—convincing the people that it should be built was another. The Barge project did not capture the popular interest as the contemporary Panama Canal did with its romance of nationalistic splendor, its vision of joining two oceans, and the enchantment of a long-distance effort. The Barge Canal, "by many and with good reason is considered a greater engineering feat than the Panama Canal, but like the prophet in his own country its home state has been foremost in failing to appreciate both its greatness and importance . . . In the early days of the Erie Canal there had been romance in the thought of connecting the inland seas with the ocean, but somehow that sentiment had worn threadbare."[3]

Nevertheless, the commercial promise of the canal outweighed its lack of romance. Shippers and business people pushed for a canal to get their goods between the Great Lakes and the sea so the railroads would not monopolize the shipping trade—keeping shipping rates down was essential if commercial enterprises in the Northeast were to remain competitive. "In none of the European countries are the distances from the interior to the sea very great. The American handicap of long hauls must be made as small as possible," one historian noted.[4]

In *Rome Haul*, Walter Edmonds describes a young man bonding to the Erie Canal as he travels its long and lively waters. As a youngster, I too was captivated by the canal; now, as an adult, I have explored the many reaches of the Barge Canal and can appreciate the diverse histories of the boats and the people whose lives it has touched. I also have been privileged to talk to many people who were proud to have worked on commercial or state boats on the Barge Canal as captains, deckhands, or family. Some recalled very different experiences from those of their parents and grandparents who worked on the nineteenth-century Erie Canal, but their attitudes toward the canal probably are much like their ancestors'. Nineteenth-century Erie boaters marveled at their "new era" of canaling; now, though the old towpath is silent, the Erie's water is still churning—but now motorboats, not wooden barges, cut through Erie's quiet veil.

A LONG HAUL

1   A Working History

"The present canal must be enlarged!" said New York Governor (and soon United States President) Theodore Roosevelt of the Erie Canal in 1900.[1] New York residents had been turning their backs on their old friend the Erie. The canal connected the cities of Albany and Buffalo, moved settlers to the West, and introduced colorful characters, including a mule named Sal. But at the turn of the century the canal's narrow, muddy ribbon of water looked hopelessly inadequate alongside the shiny railroad tracks of its chief competitor.

To be competitive with the railroads, the canal had to modernize. But how do you bring a nineteenth-century canal into the twentieth century? People had learned a great deal about building canals between the construction of the first Erie and its twentieth-century descendent. Before the canal, people often moved goods along waterways such as the Mohawk River in spring high water (though sometimes the water became *too* high and *too* fast); through the rest of the year, the lack of a dependable and sufficient depth slowed or grounded their vessels. The Erie Canal avoided these unpredictable natural waterways with a hand-dug trench; the Barge Canal reverted to using the natural corridors of rivers and lakes, along with a few wide, machine-excavated channels.

Though they both crossed New York State—connecting the Hudson River to Lake Erie—the Barge Canal is a deeper, wider, updated version of the earlier waterway. A freight boat pulled by a team along the Erie Canal in 1825 would move about 30 tons at a time through 83 locks; on the Barge Canal, a self-propelled barge could carry 3,000 tons across the state through just 36 locks. With less than half the number of locks, the Barge moved boats carrying 100 times more.

There also was something different about the boats on the Barge Canal. No longer were they pulled by horses or mules walking alongside on a towpath. This new canal required that the boats either be self-propelled or pulled by tugboats. Often, tugboats

Opposite:
The Erie Barge Canal crosses New York in a canalized section of the Mohawk River as shown in this view, looking east of Lock 17 at Little Falls in the 1930s.
New York State Archives

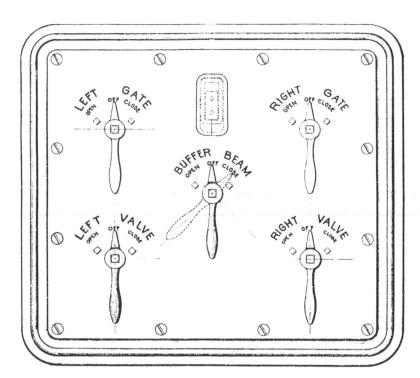

The lock operator's control stand has a panel with brass levers on this design, taken from the engineer's plans for Contract No. 92.

New York State Canal Corporation

What's In a Name?

CLINTON'S DITCH
The Erie Canal completed in 1825 under Governor DeWitt Clinton was often scornfully referred to as a ditch by those who thought the construction was a mistake. The first Erie Canal was 4 feet deep and 40 feet wide. Boats could carry about 30 tons of cargo.

ENLARGED ERIE CANAL
The Erie Canal was enlarged to 70 feet wide and 7 feet deep along its entire length by 1862 in a project that began in 1835.

ERIE BARGE CANAL
Begun in 1903 and completed in 1918, this generation of the Erie Canal is still in operation. It uses canalized lakes and rivers along with artificial channels.

pulled or pushed several barges at a time. To accommodate these larger boats, the locks on the Barge Canal were built considerably wider and deeper than in any previous canal. A lock tender on the old Erie moved large balance beams by hand to open and close the gates on 90-foot-long by 15-foot-wide locks; a Barge Canal lock operator turns small brass handles that direct electric motors to move gates on the 328-foot-long by 45-foot-wide locks.

The Barge Canal System was such an engineering marvel when it was being built between 1903 and 1918 that it frequently was compared to the impressive Panama Canal, which was being constructed at approximately the same time with much more publicity. The Barge Canal, however, is *ten times* longer than the Panama Canal and includes many more structures, some equally world famous.

The Barge Canal is following New York into the twenty-first century, as well. A lock or dam today probably runs with much the same machinery it had when it was first built. The four canals of the Barge system—the Erie, Champlain, Oswego, and Cayuga and Seneca—are sparkling gems for citizens and visitors of New York State. They have weathered well many changes in uses and operations, gaining a patina of familiarity that welcomes young and old.

It was May 15, 1918, when the Barge Canal was completed enough so that a boat could go through its entire length. Many

parts of the new canal actually had been in use for several years; completed sections were added to the system piece by piece. Among the earliest products shipped on the Barge were gravel and lumber used to complete its construction.

This transition from using animal-towed boats on the old canal to using barges and tugs on the Barge Canal is described well in Richard Garrity's *Canal Boatman: My Life on Upstate Waterways*. Garrity's father hauled lumber on the Enlarged Erie Canal for a number of years before the business began to slack off in 1909. His father heard in 1910 that "there was need for a number of Erie Canal boats to haul the thousands of cubic yards of gravel required to build the rest of the locks, concrete docks, retaining walls, bridge abutments, and culverts that were still to be constructed in many places along the Barge Canal route."[2] Garrity sold the mules and prepared to have the family's boat towed on the canal by a tug. With the change, Garrity did not have to hire his own help to unload the boat anymore—steam-powered derricks equipped with buckets did the work, along with contractor-hired labor, mostly recent Italian immigrants.

Cal Pendergrass, lock operator at Erie Barge Canal Lock 17 in the 1970s, remembered his father, also a lock operator, describing the early Barge days when there were still some barges left over from the Enlarged Erie. Cal recollected the last years of the wooden commercial boats on the Barge Canal in the 1950s,

The Barge Canal abandoned the use of animal-towed boats, so common in the nineteenth century. No towpath was constructed for the new canal. Tugboats were needed to pull the barges, which were often grouped into fleets. Here the steam tug *Sterling* pulls a fleet of five barges in the Mohawk Valley around 1936. Notice the laundry on the line on the tugboat.   *New York State Archives*

This group in 1922 is unloading wood pulp from a barge at the Barge Canal Terminal in Albany along the Hudson River.

New York State Archives

before all barge construction changed to steel. "There were a few, Feeney out of Kingston, and this *Frank Lowery* was about the last. They were just about to change over from the barges to your fleets of boats to your pushers."

The biggest problem facing the Barge when it opened was a lack of vessels designed to take advantage of the larger locks and channels the new canal offered. By the time the Barge neared completion, the nation was involved in World War I and boat-building materials were needed for the war effort—just getting essential supplies through to the canal builders was a challenge at times. To make sure supplies were getting from factories to the army overseas, the federal government took over the major transportation networks—the railroads and the canals. Canal promoters first saw this as a great boost for business—the government needed big boats and had them built. Those who supported the canal were thrilled. The federal government, they hoped, would direct shipments on the canal that might otherwise go by rail.

Such high hopes by New Yorkers, however, were not entirely fulfilled. The government did take control of most of the vessels already on the canal, and it did build a few new ones. In general, however, railroads were used wherever possible (which probably is not surprising, since former railroad officials headed the federal canal-operation effort from 1918 to 1921). Even when the war was over, the federal government did not immediately give up its

A LONG HAUL

control of traffic on the canal. As a result, commerce on the waterway was slow to increase against federally subsidized competition. During three years of operation, the federal government ran 95 boats of its own, including 20 steel steamers, 51 barges, 21 concrete barges, and 3 wooden barges.[3] Afterward, many government barges were bought by private concerns.

Concrete was used for hull construction during the war because steel was scarce due to critical wartime needs. The use of structural concrete was novel at the time and engineers tried it in many creative ways. These floating hulks weighed 267 tons empty. They could carry about 500 tons each within their 150- by 21- by 12-foot dimensions. They cost $25,000 each and were constructed in 1918 at Fort Edward, Tonawanda, Ithaca, and Detroit. Each barge was poured in one operation using 120 yards of concrete. Launching came two to four weeks later. (The time-consuming part of the construction involved making the forms, then putting wooden fittings into the barge when it was completed. The barge holds had wooden floors with wood linings.)

But the use of concrete as a hull material never caught on — the barges were easily damaged and were too heavy in the water. One of the barges, loaded with 15,000 bushels of wheat, sank at the Tonawanda dock in 1919 not long after being launched. "It appears that the barge came in contact with a bridge pier just before docking, which may have punched a hole in the shell."[4]

The *Frank A. Lowery* pulls a barge out of Lock 2 in Waterford around 1936. Built in 1918, the *Frank A. Lowery* was one of the last wooden commercial boats on the Barge Canal. Known as a *hoodledasher*, it had its own engine and could pull barges like a tug but it also had room for freight of its own.

Canal Society of New York State

The federal government built 21 concrete barges in 1918 while it controlled commerce on the Barge Canal during World War I. Wooden forms were built, then concrete was poured into the forms to build the 150-foot-long barges. This view shows three concrete barges in stages of construction at Fort Edward on Roger's Island, across from Champlain Barge Lock 7.

Canal Society of New York State
(Gayer Collection)

The barges were commercially used for just three or four years. Some of them were later deliberately sunk for use in creating better approach walls at various locks. Remains of the concrete hulks can be seen today at Erie Lock 9 at Rotterdam Junction and at Erie Lock 13 in Randall, especially during the winter, when water levels are low. (When the canal is open and the water is dammed up, little can be seen except the yellow snubbing posts resting on the hulls.) There are also some remnants (no longer visible) below the Troy Federal Lock.

When the federal government controlled the canals, the waterways carried war orders of knit goods and grain. War craft such as submarine chasers, mine layers, and mine sweepers that were built at inland shipyards used the canal to reach the seaboard. Some submarine chasers were constructed at Clayton, New York, in the Thousand Islands region of the St. Lawrence River. In 1917 the vessels were brought along Lake Ontario to Oswego, then through the Barge Canal to Albany and New York

City. The person who escorted the submarine chasers said, "The canal and locks are a wonderful piece of work, as near perfection as possible to make it." He said that his company was going to produce barges when wood became available after the war, so impressed was he with the canal system.[5]

By 1920, a variety of new shipping was developing. Imported flaxseed for linseed oil was introduced. A grain elevator completed in Brooklyn that year encouraged more grain shipments; pulpwood, rubber, and coal also made stronger appearances. The canal proved to be valuable for carrying not only bulk freight but for sensitive shipments as well—perishable items such as apples, onions, and potatoes were handled in 1920. A cargo of live eels went from Quebec to Oswego to New York City though the Barge Canal; later, eel shipments went by way of the Champlain Canal.

By 1921, grain shipments had increased 200 percent, providing a taste of the traffic seen in later years. Corn, oats, rye, barley,

When World War I ended, concrete barges such as this brand new one built by the federal government in 1918 were not wanted on the Barge Canal. A number of the barges were sunk in the Mohawk as approach walls for the locks. They can be seen today at Locks 9 and 13 on the Erie Barge Canal in the winter when the river is low. In this view, *US 114* is below Erie Lock 2 in Waterford.

New York State Museum (Scothon Collection)

The Gowanus Bay grain elevator in Brooklyn was part of the state's effort to encourage grain shipping on the Barge Canal. The elevator provided a public place to store grain before it was shipped to market. This is the elevator in 1922 shortly after it was built.

New York State Archives

and wheat eventually accounted for 75 percent of the grain trade on the Barge Canal. While only 60,000 tons of grain moved on the canal 1918, 1.2 million tons were shipped by 1931, the peak year.[6] Other items that made noticeable appearances in 1921 were brick, phosphate rock, nitrate of soda, crude sulfur, and automobiles.[7]

The Standard Oil Company that year began using motorships to transport oil. The self-propelled vessels utilized diesel engines and were much larger than the barges of the old canal—one new tanker completely filled the larger Barge Canal lock. Because of their size and engines, the motorships operated on the Great Lakes and Atlantic Coast as well as the thread between, and oil became the most important item shipped on the canal, making up 79 percent of the canal's traffic in 1950.[8] The canal thus was off and running once the federal government finally released control of it in 1921.

Not seen much when the canal was opened (especially compared to their prevalence today) were pleasure boats and people on the canal "just for fun." The canal was very much a commercial waterway up until the 1970s, when cargo traffic began to fade so much that pleasure boats became relatively more numerous than commercial barges. By then companies had found other ways to transport their products: Pipelines carried oil directly to the cities; the St. Lawrence Seaway allowed access to the Great Lakes without going through the Barge Canal; highways were improved so that trucks could move quickly on them and carry heavier loads. Shipping companies were reluctant to maintain large inventories at many points along the canal, an inherent problem when barges delivered relatively huge amounts of one item. Products could now be delivered by alternative means on a moment's notice, winter or summer. Today, commercial barges are seldom seen on the canal.

With the transition from shipping corridor to recreational waterway, the Barge Canal has adapted. Instead of factory-like warehouses at cities and towns, a traveler now sees marinas and tourist tie-ups, like the rest areas on the Thruway. In fact, the New York State Thruway Authority has operated the Barge Canal since 1992 and is attempting to make the Barge Canal a recreational waterway for visitors and weekend boaters. "We are trying to make it as user-friendly as we can," says John Jermano, former operational director of the Thruway's Canal Corporation. (Jermano retired in 1995 after ten years with canals, first under

Pleasure boats made up a greater percentage of traffic on the canal as it aged, as seen in this 1962 view of Champlain Canal Lock 5.
New York State Archives

the New York State Department of Transportation and then with the Thruway Authority.)

Today, easy-to-use ropes dangle inside the locks so recreational boaters can just grab the rope rather than having to tie up to posts like a commercial barge needs to do when the lock is filling or emptying. Bike trails, village parks and lock picnic areas make the canal more like a vacation getaway instead of the grimy channel for commercial boats it once was. In the stretch in Wayne County, for example, the canal once ran red from the waste of the beet factory in Lyons. Other industrial wastes were substantially more harmful, such as the PCB-laden sediment in portions of the Champlain Canal that resulted from an electric company's unregulated dumping. In the days before regulated septic tanks, you could tell it was washday in the villages along the canal because of the soap foam that would form at the dams from wastewater being emptied directly into the canal.[9] "In the '60s, they were able to stop point-source pollution of the canal," Jermano says. "The waters are cleaner. Because the waters are cleaner, people are coming back. Fishing is coming back."[10]

Exactly what are all these recreational boaters coming back to? The Barge Canal System consists of four different canals: The *Erie Barge Canal* follows the general route of the original Erie Canal from the Hudson River to Lake Erie; the *Champlain Barge Canal* connects Lake Champlain to the Erie Canal near Troy; the *Oswego Barge Canal* connects Lake Ontario to the Erie Canal near Syracuse; and the *Cayuga and Seneca Barge Canal* connects those two Finger Lakes to the Erie west of Syracuse. Together, the Barge Canal System includes more than 500 miles of inland waterways.

One of the biggest struggles with such a complex waterway is maintaining enough (but not too much) water throughout the system. The mandated depth of the Champlain, Cayuga and

The Barge Canal Today

CANAL	LOCATION	LENGTH	LOCKS
Erie	Waterford to Tonawanda	340 miles	36
Champlain	Troy to Whitehall	63 miles	11
Cayuga and Seneca	Montezuma to Seneca Lake	27 miles[11]	4
Oswego	Three Rivers to Oswego	24 miles	7

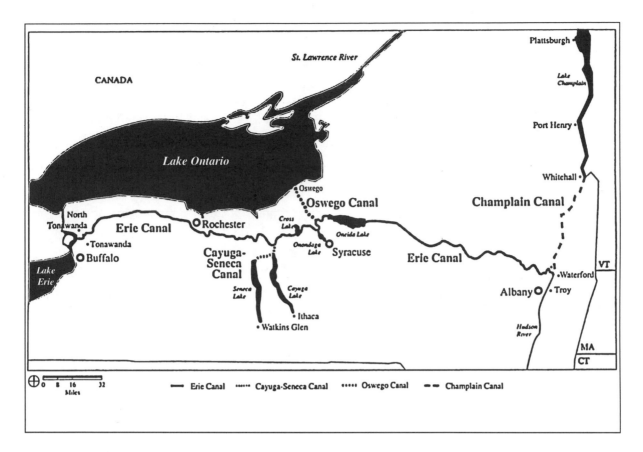

Seneca, and the Erie Barge Canal west of Three Rivers is 12 feet. From that last location east to Waterford, the depth on the Erie is 14 feet. The Oswego Canal also has a 14-foot depth. The water levels are maintained with locks and dams and by dredging the channels.

There are 58 *lift locks* on the Barge Canal system, which act like stairs to different levels of the canal. On the Barge, locks raise or lower boats anywhere from 6 to 40.5 feet; most have a lift between 16 and 20 feet. (Lock 32, in Pittsford, for example, has a 25-foot lift and holds 2.7 million gallons of water in its chamber. The shorter upper gates weigh about 50 tons while the lower ones weigh about 100 tons.)[12]

The process of emptying and filling the locks involves much that can't be seen from above. Well below the top and within the lock wall is a tunnel running the length of the lock on both sides. At each end, the tunnel is shuttered with valves that raise or lower the water. From these tunnels are windows or ports that connect the tunnels with the bottom of the lock chamber. If the lock needs to be filled (to raise a boat), the lock gates are closed and water from the higher side of the lock is let through the tunnels and ports into the lock chamber. If the lock needs to be

Map of New York State Canal System.
Beyer Blinder Belle Consortium. Courtesy New York State Recreationway Plan

emptied (to lower a boat), water is let out of the lock through the ports, into the tunnels, and is released downstream. Once the desired level is attained, the gates open and the boat proceeds to the new level. The gates and the valves are operated by seven-horsepower electric motors (about the power of a garden-tractor engine). Originally, power for the machinery and lights at the locks was generated in the white, concrete powerhouses still located at some locks.

Some locks work in conjunction with adjoining dams. There are two main types of dams on the canal. A *fixed dam* is a conventional structure that holds back a set volume of water behind a stationary wall. Some dams on the canal, though, are *adjustable* or *movable*: They are taken completely out of the water in winter. They hold back water in large pools when the canal is open; in winter the dam's walls are lifted out of the water so the river can resume its natural course. The most noticeable movable dams on the canal are on the Mohawk River. There are about 40 major dams visible to boaters on the Barge Canal system.

In addition, more then 300 highway or railroad bridges cross the canal. Most are stationary—the deck of the bridge is built at

The gates at Lock 6 on the Champlain Canal in Fort Miller are controlled by 7-horsepower motors. The powerhouse for the lock is on the right. The water in the lock is low, waiting for a boat coming from the lower level. Water behind the upper gates is 16.5 feet higher than the water in the lock and at the lower level. This is a c.1918 view of the lock, looking north.

Canal Society of New York State

A LONG HAUL

the level of the adjoining banks. A handful, though, are *lift bridges*—when a barge or boat approaches, an operator raises the bridge high enough above the water so a boat can pass.

Other noteworthy features of the canal are the *guard gates*. Looking something like guillotines, the steel gates hang over the canal, held up by towers on each side (sometimes with the additional support of a tower midway in the channel—the boats would travel on either side of the center support). If there is a break in the canal, an operator lowers the guard gate in order to stop water from draining out—an important safety check. The guard gates also are used to close off a section of canal so that it can be drained and repaired, especially in the off season. Guard gates are placed about every 10 miles on the artificial (*land-line*) sections of the canal.

The challenges of operating a canal with such diverse structures (some of them 80 years old) are numerous. The canal is carefully inspected every spring and fall by engineers and maintenance supervisors, who rate 40 separate items at each structure. They are most concerned that the machinery is correctly maintained because much of it cannot easily be replaced. "I defy anyone to see 1918 equipment still in use today

Movable dams, such as is shown in this c.1935 view of the one in Tribes Hill, allow water to be held behind the dam to form a deeper pool for boats to clear the river bottom. Erie Lock 12 allows boats to go around the dam.

New York State Archives

The Lock Hall of Fame

MOST PHOTOGRAPHED

In Lockport, the original Erie Canal required a pair of five joined locks to lift boats up the Niagara Escarpment to the level of Lake Erie. These were replaced by an equal number of larger locks during the first enlargement. The Barge Canal accomplished the lift with two still larger locks; the northern half of the nineteenth-century enlarged locks remain alongside.

MOST CELEBRATED ACHIEVEMENT

In Waterford, five Erie Barge Canal locks lift boats 169 feet in a mile and a half. These locks have lifts from 32.5 to 34.5 feet. There are short pools between the locks to store water for and from the lockings. The five Barge Canal locks replaced the 16 locks of the Enlarged Erie, which went down the opposite shore of the Mohawk through Cohoes.

HIGHEST LIFT

In Little Falls, Erie Lock 17 lifts boats 40.5 feet, the highest lift of any Barge Canal lock. When it was built, it was the highest lift lock in the world. The eastern end of the lock has a drop, guillotine-like gate instead of the horizontal-swing miter gates used on other locks.

MOST UNUSUAL ENGINEERING

In Oswego, Lock 8 of the Oswego Barge Canal links the canal with Lake Ontario. It originally was a siphon lock that used air instead of electricity to fill and empty the lock, the first such lock built in the United States.

in this good shape," Jermano says, referring to the operating machinery on the Barge.[13]

The Canal Corporation tries to keep the canal operating while maintaining the waterway's historical significance. For instance, a few locks are repaired each year according to a systematic schedule; the work includes mending the concrete, repairing the gates, and generally refurbishing the lock. However, before it does these projects, the maintenance staff consults with the New York State Department of Parks, Recreation, and Historic Preservation. Previously, changes were made to the canal with less regard for its historic importance. Small repairs—such as removing the original cast-concrete stairways at the locks, replacing the lift-bridge control houses, and modernizing the control lights at the locks—did not seem to alter the functioning of the canal. As the locks began to buy electricity instead of generating it on site, some of the stately powerhouses were demolished. Jermano looks back with regret on those losses. "I feel bad we tore down some of the powerhouses. But we stopped what we were doing . . . destroying things. Now we are preserving the best of the past. People are extremely proud of what we are doing," he says.[14]

The Canal Corporation also must be concerned with current environmental issues. One of the big problems is dredging. A dredge scoops or sucks mud or debris from the bottom of the canal or river to keep the channels deep enough for boats to navigate, a particularly hard chore where streams or rivers empty into the canal and dump mud and sand from upstream. (For example, where the Genesee River crosses the Barge Canal near Rochester, dredges remove an estimated 25,000 cubic yards of silt each year—about as much as 1,000 dump trailers would hold.)[15]

Dredging permits must be obtained from the New York State Department of Environmental Conservation and the United States Army Corps of Engineers, the agencies that oversee water quality. Dredging in the canal stirs up silt that can make the water cloudy and more difficult for fish to live in. But the dredging budget in recent years has not kept pace with the needs of the canal. Consequently, a 14-foot depth between the Hudson River and Lake Ontario has been difficult to guarantee, and much of the canal will be dredged over the next few years to make sure that the deeper-draft boats it was designed for can comfortably navigate the waterway.

Other maintenance on the canal is undertaken in the winter, when the canal is empty of both water and traffic. The canal is closed usually by the first of December and preparations are made for the harsh upstate winter: The water in the land-line

This powerhouse at Erie Barge Lock 13 on the Mohawk River still looks new in this c.1918 view.

Canal Society of New York State

channels is drawn down by opening dams and closing off water sources such as Lake Erie so that just a narrow stream of water remains; the guard gates around the Genesee River in Rochester are dropped; and the movable dams in the Mohawk River are raised to let the river flow through its natural course.

Once the water is drained, the work begins. The machinery that operates the gates and locks is sometimes taken apart for preventive maintenance. Many parts still date from the original construction and cannot now be purchased, at any price, anywhere—replacements are made from scratch. With the water level lowered, a detailed inspection of the system can take place. At locks to be worked on, a *coffer dam* (a temporary dam made of wood or metal that is put next to the lock to cut it off from the water still in the canal) is installed and the water pumped out of the lock, making the lock chamber accessible to construction equipment. Large cranes are sometimes used to adjust and balance the gates (each gate weighs at least 50 tons). The gates might be sandblasted and repainted. New wooden quoin posts and seals are placed, and cracked or chipped concrete walls are repaired. (Pre-cast concrete panels are now sometimes used to repair the walls.)

Maintenance activities take place at the canal shops in the winter. This state derrick boat crew at the Utica Section Shop in the 1940s is preparing to raise a winch, probably from the derrick boat.

New York State Thruway, Canal Corporation

Besides the large repair projects that take place each winter, operators at the locks and dams perform smaller-scale but no less vital maintenance. They take the control boards and motors inside and disassemble them for cleaning and inspection, replacing worn parts. When boats are coming through the locks during the season, lock operators do not have time for such traffic-stopping activities.

There is also winter activity at the canal maintenance shops in Fort Edward, Waterford, Fonda, Utica, Syracuse, Lyons, Pittsford, Albion, and Lockport. These shops have customized machinery for making and repairing needed parts. For example, in Waterford the five-ton valves that control the water flowing into and out of the tunnels within the lock walls are rebuilt. They require brass bushings to allow the valves' wheels to move smoothly on their tracks. These bushings are individually made at the shops. In the carpentry shop at Waterford, wooden patterns are kept for every quoin post for every lock. Each one has a slightly different shape; each needs to be custom cut from white oak.

Another major winter repair is the maintenance of the state's work boats—the dredges, tugboats, derrick boats, tenders, and

The state tug *Syracuse* is in the Waterford dry dock around 1925 for maintenance or winter storage.
New York State Museum (Scothon Collection)

buoy boats—all easily identified by their bright blue-and-yellow paint scheme. Some of the fleet is as old as the Barge Canal itself. Like the locks, the vessels need careful maintenance. The propellers, gears, and drive shafts are reconditioned, and worn or rusted parts of the exteriors of the vessels are repaired and painted.

The canal generally opens again around the first of May. Water is let into the canal about two or three weeks before the canal is formally opened in order to let state crews set the buoys that mark the navigable channel in the river and lake sections. (Red buoys are always on the right going away from the ocean; green is on the left.)

Once the canal is open, boaters have the opportunity to ply any of the more than 500 miles of Barge Canal waterway. Each part of the canal has its own distinctive features. For instance, the Cayuga and Seneca Barge Canal connects the two Finger Lakes of the same names, thus creating nearly a hundred miles of navigable water. The canal includes a set of *tandem* or *joined locks* in picturesque Seneca Falls. Birds abound on this canal, which begins near the rustic charm of the Montezuma Wildlife Preserve, cuts south 4.5 miles to Cayuga Lake, then goes west to Seneca Falls, Waterloo, and Seneca Lake. Beacons in the lakes mark the channels to the southern ends of Cayuga Lake (Ithaca) and Seneca Lake (Watkins Glen).

(Watkins Glen contains probably the most forgotten portion of the Barge Canal system. A stretch of the old Chemung Canal from the lake to Montour Falls still falls within the jurisdiction of the Canal Corporation. Frequented by pleasure boaters today, this short waterway is interesting to canal historians, since it may have survived as a relic of a grand plan to rebuild the entire Chemung Canal during the construction of the Barge Canal. The plan never went much beyond the drafting table.)

The Oswego Barge Canal links Lake Ontario to the Erie Canal at Three Rivers Point, just west of Oneida Lake, where the Seneca, Oneida, and Oswego Rivers join. (The canal is in the Oswego River for the most part.) At almost all the locks there are dams with adjoining hydroelectric power plants. The canal continues north through Phoenix, Fulton, and Oswego, a busy route since colonial days because of its connection to the Great Lakes. When Oswego Barge Canal Lock 8 was built, it was one of only two siphon-powered locks in the world. A *siphon lock* uses the movement of air (rather than electrically operated valves) to fill and empty the lock. The siphon at Lock 8 was replaced with more traditional machinery in 1968.[16]

The Champlain Barge Canal connects the Hudson River to Lake Champlain at Whitehall and has a now non-navigable spur to Glens Falls (the Glens Falls Feeder). The beauty of the Adirondacks and the heritage of Revolutionary War sites add special character to this canal.

The Erie Barge Canal generally follows the corridor of the original nineteenth-century Erie Canal. The exceptions are largely due to the decision of the Barge's planners to use canalized rivers and lakes where possible, a decision that went against the practice of the nineteenth-century canal builders to avoid the then-unmanageable waterways. The canal is connected to Lake Erie by the Niagara River. Instead of its nineteenth-century terminus at Buffalo, the Canal's official western entrance now does not start until Tonawanda Creek. Leaving the creek at Pendleton, the canal uses an artificial channel that was first dug for the original Erie, but which is now widened, straightened, and deepened nearly to Rochester. The overlap of several generations of Erie Canals is striking at Lockport, where the locks of the Enlarged Erie survive along with their Barge Canal replacements. West of Rochester, the Barge Canal loops south of the city (instead of going through it, as its famous predecessor did); it reconnects with the old canal route near Pittsford. From

Opposite:
An aerial view of the canal in Waterloo shows the elements of the power generating at that site. Lock 4 on the Cayuga and Seneca Canal is on the left. Water is directed around the lock with the loop on the right. At the end of the loop is the New York State Electric and Gas power plant. In the island in the middle is the substation that transfers power from the plant to power lines.   *New York State Electric and Gas*

A LONG HAUL

there to Lyons, the Barge Canal continues along the Erie's 1825 route, often paralleling the original route as it weaves in and out of Ganargua Creek. East of Lyons, the canal uses a series of natural waterways, including the Clyde, Seneca, and Oneida Rivers, and Oneida Lake. It skirts north of the original canal route that went through Port Byron, Jordan, Syracuse, Fayetteville, and Durhamville. East of Oneida Lake, the canal is in a land line until reaching the Mohawk River at Rome; except for a few sections, the Mohawk continues the canal to Waterford, where another short land line takes it around Cohoes Falls. The land line at Waterford brings the canal down to the Hudson River through a series of five dramatic locks.

Major uses of canal water now include more than just transportation, and these other uses sometimes compete with each another. The Barge Canal system helps regulate the water levels in adjoining rivers and lakes. After the navigation season ends in the late fall, many of the system's water sources (such as the reservoirs) are purposely lowered in expectation of spring flooding—the system can then better assimilate the extra water from snowmelt and spring rains without flooding.

Recreational boating, fishing, swimming, and water skiing are now important activities on the canal. A 1993 report prepared for the Canal Corporation by the United States Geological Survey outlined these and other trends. "The number of summer cottages and year-round homes along shores is increasing, as are the number of marinas, state and municipal parks, boat ramps and campgrounds."[17] Homes, industries, and businesses use the canal as a water supply; the canal also is an outlet for treated sewage or for industrial waste water, as well as a home to fish and other wildlife. The report explains, "Water-level regulation on some lakes by other agencies poses a possible threat to marshes and trout habitat when lake levels are altered to satisfy navigation needs or other requirements. For example, the winter drawdowns on certain lakes need to be limited to meet spawning requirements."[18] Canal water is also used to generate power and to irrigate nearby farms. All of these non-navigation uses of the canal (including constructing camps along it) require permits from the state.

The Barge Canal is often referred to as living history because so many remnants of its nineteenth-century predecessors are easily visible today. Some serve only as reminders of past eras and past lives—the still-noble arches of the 1856 Montezuma Aqueduct of the Enlarged Erie Canal cannot be passed unobserved by boaters on today's Barge Canal. But the working

part of the Barge Canal system includes a network of reservoirs and dams constructed in the mid-nineteenth century that remain important today, including North and South Lakes in northern Herkimer County, or Lake Moraine, near Hamilton. Their histories are in many ways distant in time and space from today's waterway, but they are nonetheless active parts of a mutually dependent system.

The memory of the canal as a vital commercial highway remains strong, especially among those who spent their working lives on it. Their descriptions offer vivid histories of what cannot be seen today, such as the fleets of working barges. "My heart has always been on the canal," said Bill Hills of his days of working the boats in the 1930s. Today's canal is the result of the vision of many generations of citizens—a vision that viewed canaling as important to both the state's commerce and its culture.

When the Barge Canal opened, it was advertised as an avenue for shipping goods. Signs like this one at Erie Barge Lock 9 in 1922 were meant to encourage shippers to consider the canal. Now the canal is being advertised as a waterway for recreational boaters.

New York State Archives

2   A Decision to Make the Erie Bigger

In 1903, shortly into the century of automobiles and airplanes, New Yorkers were asked to sink a lot of money into a better canal system for their state. Yes, New York had become the Empire State partly because of its canal system of the previous century, but did that mean that canals were still the way to go? Not everyone agreed they were. Even though cargo could still travel cheaply by canal boat, people were not sure they should invest so much money to enlarge and maintain a canal. There was a desperate need for better roads as the automobile era was unfolding and railroads appeared to be a more efficient, or at least a more modern, cargo carrier.

"The real issue upon which the people are called upon to voice their opinion is to whether they shall vote $101 million, to say nothing of interest charges, in order to build a *shallow, old fashioned tow-line barge canal* between the Great Lakes and the sea," said a writer for the *Fairport Herald* in 1903.[1] Fairport would remain on the canal and would seem to have much to gain from a bigger canal. If the citizens in Fairport were not for it, who was?

The businesses that used the canal to ship their products were strongly in favor of improving the canal. Shippers in New York City and Buffalo especially had a lot to gain from the project. Many thought that about 75 percent of what would be carried on the improved canal would be grain from the Midwest farm belt. That grain would end up in New York City—specifically in the hands of the New York Produce Exchange, to be distributed through its network of agriculture-based businesses. New York businesses started talking about an improved waterway when much of the rest of the state had given up on canals. They wanted an enlarged canal that would allow bigger boats to move faster—after all, they were competing with the faster and continually improving railroads. The canals were also vying for their place in a shipping world that would soon see goods moved by trucks on publicly subsidized roads.

Opposite:
On the right lock wall of this 1909 construction view of Champlain Lock 11 at Comstock the round portholes are clearly visible. Most likely, these workers were recent Italian immigrants.

New York State Archives

Both a canal barge and a railroad engine are stopped alongside of the Barge Canal Terminal in Buffalo around 1920. With two competing routes for goods, Barge Canal advocates claimed freight rates in New York State would be kept low.

New York State Museum
(Scothon Collection)

The Erie Canal had seen previous enlargements. Completed in 1825, it was originally four feet deep, then deepened to seven feet by 1862. In the nineteenth century, canal craft went from 30-ton capacity to 300 tons. The Erie had been in a constant state of improvement since its construction; an observer noted in 1909 that "just at what point the pending project became distinctively a barge canal would be difficult to fix." The Barge Canal was "not the product of a revolution but rather of a gradual evolution."[2]

In 1884, a series of improvements began that lead directly to the Barge Canal as we know it today. The lock-lengthening program doubled the length of one of the two chambers of the locks on the Enlarged Erie Canal so barges could be locked through two at a time. In 10 years, 52 locks were lengthened.[3]

The infamous "Nine-Million-Dollar Improvement" was begun in 1895. The purpose of this project was to make the canal two feet deeper and to raise the bridges so that higher loaded boats could pass. Unfortunately, the $9 million budgeted for the deepening project was not enough, even if the work had gone as predicted, and many recognized this fact at the time. Compounding the problem was that dishonest contractors were getting more than their share of the money. Work was halted at the end of 1897 with less than two-thirds of the job completed. Suspicions were cast toward everyone connected with the canal,

and the state was left with an only partially deepened waterway. "The question naturally arose whether to continue the nine-foot deepening or provide for a larger canal."[4]

The suggestion was made that the state needed to go to a far more ambitious plan and build a ship canal that would allow ocean-going vessels access through New York State to the Great Lakes. Such a waterway would need to be at least 20 feet deep, with a width that would have forced the relocation of many homes and industries in the canal corridor. The idea already had been discussed for several decades. The federal government spent almost half a million dollars in 1897 to create the "Deep Waterways Survey" of possible locations for such a canal. But when the survey and accompanying report were presented to Congress in 1900, the conclusion was that a ship canal would not be as useful for New York State as a smaller, barge-oriented canal would be.[5] The report stated that it seemed impossible that a boat could be built strong enough for ocean travel yet inexpensively enough to make lake and canal travel economical. The federal survey for the ship canal was nonetheless useful in determining the eventual Barge Canal route.

With the ship canal now moot, Governor Roosevelt considered the Barge Canal option in light of new roads and a spreading rail network. "New York has certain topographic advantages which it would be folly not to utilize," Roosevelt's

An overview of Erie Basin in Buffalo in 1920 shows a busy place. Between the Barge Canal terminal building in the center of the picture and the frame warehouse in the foreground, a number of wooden barges are tied up.

New York State Archives

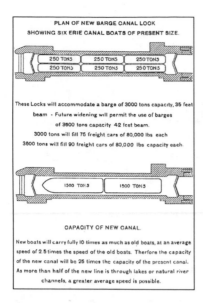

PLAN OF NEW BARGE CANAL LOOK
SHOWING SIX ERIE CANAL BOATS OF PRESENT SIZE.

250 TONS | 250 TONS | 250 TONS
250 TONS | 250 TONS | 250 TONS

These Locks will accommodate a barge of 3000 tons capacity, 35 feet
beam - Future widening will permit the use of barges
of 3600 tons capacity 42 feet beam.
3000 tons will fill 75 freight cars of 80,000 lbs each
3600 tons will fill 90 freight cars of 80,000 lbs capacity each.

1500 TONS | 1500 TONS

CAPACITY OF NEW CANAL.

New boats will carry fully 10 times as much as old boats, at an average
speed of 2.5 times the speed of the old boats. Therefore the capacity
of the new canal will be 25 times the capacity of the present canal.
As more than half of the new line is through lakes or natural river
channels, a greater average speed is possible.

This page from the 1914 *Barge Canal Bulletin*, written by the state engineer to promote the Barge Canal project, shows how shipping would be improved by the Barge Canal. *New York State Library*

appointed Committee on Canals reported.[6] The committee explained that New York had the best water route for shipping of any state, and that New York City would lose its shipping advantage if it depended solely on railroads, since railroads were common at other port cities as well. Roosevelt energetically called the state into action to improve its canals, and he is credited with taking the initial step both with this canal and later (as president) with the Panama Canal.[7]

In 1900 the governor signed a law requesting the state engineer to make the necessary surveys and estimates for construction and for improving the Erie, Champlain, and Oswego Canals. The state engineer at the time, Edward Bond, faced a massive job. The surveys had to be done in just 10 months—in time to report to the legislature at the beginning of the 1901 session—and the information had to be as accurate as if construction had been actually ordered.

Bond recognized the challenge when he said in his 1900 annual report, "The plans for this work shall be so thoroughly considered and that the estimates of costs for its various portions shall be agreed upon by so many well-known and experienced engineers . . . that they shall command the confidence of the public and will enable the legislature and the people of the State to form a full and unbiased judgment as to the desirability of building this great canal."[8]

He knew many people had lost confidence in canals by this time (on the heels of the failure of the Nine-Million-Dollar Improvement), so he was determined to produce such a well-researched document that the people would once again believe in the usefulness of canals for New York State. His report included detailed maps and drawings of proposed structures, possible routes, water supply systems, and cost comparisons for nearly everything.

For example, for the problem of trying to get the canal up the steep elevation caused by the falls near Cohoes, Bond wrote, "The ascent of the canal around the falls of the Mohawk River at Cohoes has been one of the most difficult problems to solve and has, therefore, received my earnest attention. First, there was the location to choose, and secondly the kinds of locks to be decided upon."[9] He considered putting in mechanical lift locks, but he did not know of any that went higher than 60 feet—and the falls at Cohoes are about 120 feet. He invited engineers to submit solutions and received plans for hydraulic and electrical locks. His advisory board of engineers considered the different types of locks as well as different routes

A LONG HAUL

around the falls. The board finally decided to go with the time-proven masonry lock, for "although the advantages of the mechanical lift are many, a proper conservatism demanded the use of the old and tried."[10] In the end, Bond's report proposed two possible routes around the falls—a route through lower Cohoes and up along the north side of the Mohawk gorge, and a route through Waterford. The latter route was the one eventually chosen and is included in the Barge Canal Law of 1903—in fact, Bond's report was the basis of the canal specifications included later in the Barge Canal Law.

While the engineers were busy with notes from the field, canal advocates were busy convincing the public of the canal's value. By the close of the 1901 legislative session there was a clearly defined group that believed the canals must be improved, but the group was divided over the extent of the improvement.

Below:
Top: Because the 1900 Bond Report was so detailed and well researched, including such drawings as this elaborate lift bridge, the report was used as the basis for the canal route as described in the 1903 Barge Canal Law.
Barge Canal Book of Plans (1920)
Bottom: As shown by this 1994 view looking west of the Fairport lift bridge, the lift bridges were not built as elaborately as the drawing.
Author's collection

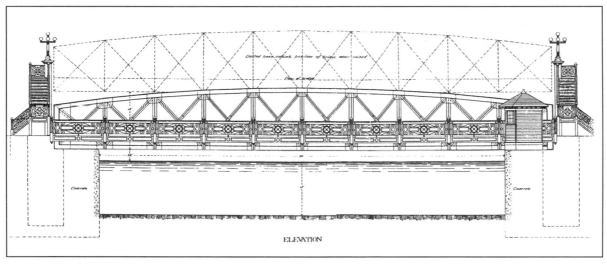

ELEVATION

Some structures from the nineteenth-century Erie were carried over to the Barge Canal. For instance, the 1850 Syracuse Weighlock Building, shown here around 1910, continued to house canal administration offices until the 1950s.   *Canal Society of New York State*

Would the state's voters approve money for the proposed 1,000-ton barge canal, or would a smaller-scale deepening project (similar to the 1895 improvement) have to be enough? New York City seemed to want the larger canal; the rest of the state appeared willing to settle for something less.

At a New York City dinner in December 1901, Andrew Carnegie made a bold announcement. He said that the Carnegie Steel Company planned to construct a $12-million plant on Lake Erie near Buffalo because he had great confidence the state would never fail to enlarge the Erie Canal. Another man at the dinner, Lewis Nixon, suggested a compromise between those who wanted the deepening project and those who wanted a 1,000-ton canal: Why not build locks with dimensions for 1,000-ton boats, but leave the prism at 9 feet? That way, he said, the canal could easily be enlarged further at a later date.[11]

Governor Benjamin Odell must have liked Nixon's idea because in his address to the 1902 legislature he suggested that plan, reducing the total number of locks from 72 to 44.[12] But the anti-canal contingent, led mostly by railroad leaders, worked just as hard against the project. The plan failed to pass the legislature.

The governor was reelected by a narrow margin that fall. Many politicians turned pro-canal to avoid losing key support and votes from an apparently increasingly pro-canal public. During the campaign, a canal route across the state to Lake Erie was accepted over a proposal that diverted the Erie Canal to Lake Ontario. The decision was not so much economic as it was political—by going across upstate, the canal would touch a good share of western New York, and thus benefit western New York voters.[13]

Anti-canal organizers developed three different plans to divert interest from the canal early in 1903. The first was to introduce a resolution to build a railway in the bed of the canal, an idea that did not get far. The second was to eliminate the section of the state constitution that forbade the state from selling, leasing, or disposing of the state canals. That idea likewise gained little support. The most unusual diversion was presented to the canal committees of the senate and assembly on March 11 by the International Towing and Power Company, which proposed placing rails on the canal towpath and using electric tractors instead of animals to tow the barges. The company claimed that goods could be transported this way for 50 cents a ton from Buffalo to Albany. (A counter argument claimed that barges were

People in Buffalo were in favor of the Barge Canal because they expected their city could become an iron and steel center. Scrap iron eventually did move to Buffalo on the Barge Canal. This load of scrap steel (possibly bomb shell casings left over from World War I) at the Lockport locks in 1921 is heading to the Lackawanna Steel Company near Buffalo.

New York State Archives

already being towed by steam canal boats for 50 cents a ton from Buffalo to New York—about 150 miles farther.) This twilight effort received only moderately more attention than the other two did.

The bill that provided for the enlargement of the Oswego, Champlain, and Erie canals to 12 feet deep at a cost of $101 million passed both the senate and the assembly in 1903; an act to authorize the state to borrow for the work then went before the voters. Citizens of the state were for or against the canal for often purely local reasons. Residents of the Mohawk Valley were concerned that changes proposed for the Mohawk River section would cause flooding; Buffalo citizens, on the other hand, favored the canal so the city might become an iron and steel center. From April 7 to November 3 the canal issue was presented in newspapers, at county fairs, and at meetings of chambers of commerce and boards of trade.

But being situated along the canal does not seem to have influenced Fairport's opposition to the canal plan. The *Fairport Herald* made it clear that the people of the town did not want the Erie enlarged through the town, even though New York City and other large cities would probably pay for most of the cost of the project. What did Fairport stand to lose in having an improved waterway at its doorstep?

An article in the October 7, 1903, *Herald* implied that the sheer cost of the project was at fault. The state had never spent that amount of money on one project; the article pointed out the cost of all public school buildings in New York State (and the land they were on) was almost $9 million less than the projected cost of the Barge Canal project. The writer objected, "We do not believe the expenditure will produce an equal return."[14]

Also, residents of Fairport, as in many other communities upstate, thought the present Erie was bad enough. They had little respect for the workers who appeared when the canal opened each spring. "The Erie Canal has not opened yet, but it is faithfully promised that the big ditch will be active soon. In the meantime, the same old bunch of canal dependents who are forever pulling their wires for a canal job are whittling another stick apiece and waiting for orders from headquarters."[15] Later that year, the *Herald* quoted the *Hornellsville Times'* plea to the voters to "not be deceived by the claim that the proposed barge canal will bring prosperity to this state or any section of it. A ship canal might do it, but a twelve foot ditch, never!"[16]

The canal issue, in fact, was probably not that important to the average person. The canal had long ceased to provide competitive passenger service, as it had with the sleek packet

boats of its early days. People did not see barges loaded with grain or other bulk items affecting them. Railroads, trolleys, or cars were another matter, however—people could directly use and enjoy those forms of transportation. As the *Herald* stated in July 1903, "A proposition to expend a large amount in the construction of good roads would be looked upon with favor by the great mass of farmers."[17]

The canal raised concern when it affected residents' own backyards. Leaving the language about the public waste of such a canal behind, the *Herald* noted that local people were most concerned that the widened canal would take their land. "Those of our citizens who chance to live in the path of the proposed waterway are a bit anxious as to where they will go for new houses."[18]

However, unlike the unfavorable press it received in Fairport, the Barge Canal proposal was well received in Rome, a traditional canal town. (The first shovel of dirt had been turned for the Erie Canal at Rome nearly a century earlier.) But other factors bolstered the town's support. Rome actually had two canals bringing commerce through the city: In addition to the old Erie, the historic Black River Canal connected Rome with the Black River to the north, and its deteriorating condition

The Barge Canal expanded the old Erie's route through Fairport despite the fact that residents were not thrilled with the project. This 1921 view shows a Cowles tug, the *Lorraine*, pulling the *I.L.I. 101*, later known as the *Day Peckinpaugh*, on its maiden voyage. The motorship, with a number of conversions, became the longest-running commercial vessel on the Barge Canal System, finally leaving the canal in 1994. *New York State Archives*

Rome citizens looked forward to the commerce the Barge Canal would bring to their city. This view of the Barge Canal Terminal at Rome in 1994 shows the motorship *Day Peckinpaugh* on its last season on the canal.

New York State Museum

affected the town. "Unless general Erie improvement is begun soon a great deal of money must be spent upon the present waterway [the Black River Canal] to replace fifty-year old structures which now are barely holding together."[19] The newspaper reported that the Erie and Black River Canals enjoyed brisk business that year, and actually had a gain in traffic from 1902.[20] The newspaper's opinion of the canal and its workers was complimentary, a far cry from Fairport's opinion of them as an "old bunch of dependents."

According to S. H. Beach, a Rome citizen who wrote a letter to the *Rome Daily Sentinel*, the new Barge Canal would bring cheap coal and other cheap raw materials to Rome manufacturing plants, and because the level of the canal would be below the present level of the roads the canal would drain swamps south of the city. Beach said the proposed route would connect Rome to Oneida Lake, "which added to the four square miles of lake formed by the proposed dam at Delta will give us long wished for water and boating privileges."[21] Rome also stood to gain from the canalization of the Mohawk River, he claimed—the taming of

One Person's Opinion

Workingmen Attention

Your brain and brawn are your capital. The capital of the business man is his money. When the later fails to find a profitable investment, the former also ceases to be employed. Public improvements are invariably profitable investments for the public capital, and must of necessity employ more or less labor according to the magnitude of the suggested improvement.

The State of New York, of which you are citizens, has decided to refer the question of the improvement of its canal, at a cost of $101,000,000 to you to decide at the next general election. If you vote Yes when the question is submitted to you, you vote to create employment for thousands of mechanics and laborers for the next five years in the various trades and callings employed in the production, construction and appliances of such material as is used in an undertaking of such description, and upon its completion the labor that would be employed in the erection of new manufacturing plants and their attendant surroundings which must follow. If you vote No upon this question you are simply voting in favor of private monopolies, who whenever opportunity presents itself, never hesitates to tax you for the necessaries of life, to the utmost limit, while it buys the labor it needs in the very cheapest market.

The Railroad monopolies, owned and controlled by such men as the Vanderbilts, Jno D. Rockfeller, J. Pierpont Morgan, Geo Gould, and that "agent of" divine providence ____ Baer are opposed to the State of New York building a barge canal, or even improving the present one. !Why! Because such a canal, owned and opperated [sic] by you, the citizens, precludes the possibility of them charging you extortionist rates for transporting the necessaries of life to the consuming centres, and gives you the possession of an effective check upon their legalized brigandage.

Think of this when you are about to cast your ballot and in self deference, you will vote for the 1000 Ton Barge Canals.

the river would stop the "now almost semi-annual serious flooding of the lower portion of the city."[22]

The *Sentinel* reassured people that the poor spending practices exposed during the Nine-Million-Dollar Improvement would not happen again. Throughout 1903, the paper published arguments in favor of the canal; at one point, the paper even suggested building the canal was more important than building a new Oneida County courthouse.[23]

The *Sentinel* also appealed to national pride: "The Erie is the longest canal in the world outside of China, and if improved as planned will be comparable with no other in the world."[24] The editors pointed out that the canal would help both farms (by carrying grain) and industry (by carrying iron).[25]

A penciled manuscript found in a copy of Bond's 1901 report.

The power generated at the canal locks and dams would benefit industry as well. "New Yorkers will be foolish to lose the prize of commerce which is implied in the new canal they are asked to provide. It will come our way if we go for it. Otherwise others will get it."[26]

One of the first promotional banquets for the Barge Canal vote was held in nearby Utica on July 28, 1903.[27] Four hundred people attended the banquet, and pro-canal speeches were printed verbatim in the *Sentinel*. The paper contrasted the energetic evening with an anti-canal convention in Rochester attended by only half as many people. (Indeed, the paper claimed many of the anti-canal group probably attended only because of the reduced-rate train tickets the railroads provided.) The paper summarized its stance by asking Rochester where it would be without the influence of the canal. "When the 1,000-ton barge waterway materializes, and Rochester grows 50 percent by reason of its running right alongside, she will be ashamed of her present attempt to bite off her own nose."[28]

However, despite the opinions expressed upstate, "the chief battle ground in this whole campaign was New York City and in the end it was New York City that carried the day," said the contemporary historian and engineer, Noble Whitford.[29] By November, canal literature was generously distributed in New York City amidst an intensive campaign of meetings. Sixty speakers worked in the campaign; literature was distributed at more than 1,000 mass meetings, on ferries, and at factories.[30]

Both sides battled down to the wire. A pro-canal letter signed by prominent business people appeared in major New York City newspapers the day before the vote. On the other side, the International Towing and Power Company, intent on proving that the canal improvement would not be needed at all if its system was constructed, demonstrated its electric "mules" in Schenectady less than a week before the vote.[31]

Despite such actions, the borrowing provisions of Chapter 147 of the Laws of 1903 were finally placed before the voters. Known as the "Barge Canal Law," the act allowed the state to borrow and spend $101 million "for the improvement of the Erie canal, the Oswego canal and the Champlain canal to allow for 1,000-ton barges." (Eventually, the system was built for 3,000-ton barges and the final cost, including the addition of the Cayuga and Seneca Canal and the Barge Canal terminals, was over $170 million.)

The Barge Canal won by earning nearly three-quarters of the 1,100,708 votes cast on November 3, 1903.[32] Greater New York voted in favor, as did Erie County and Buffalo at the western end.

Other counties in favor included Albany, Essex, Herkimer, Nassau, Niagara, Orleans, Rockland, Schenectady, Suffolk, and Ulster. Monroe County, Fairport's home, went 16,000 votes against it. The *Fairport Herald* used just a few column inches to describe the favorable vote.[33]

New York City carried the canal vote. One proud New York City writer dubbed his town the "Sovereign City" and said that "if every canal county above the Bronx had reversed its majority, so that the city stood alone against all the rest of the state, the proposition would still have been carried by over 150,000. Thus the metropolis is already able to impose its will upon the state."[34]

The vote to improve the Erie Canal and the laterals confirmed the state's commitment to transporting 1,000-ton canal barges across the state. The victory ushered in a new era of canal building, a task so immense that engineers esteemed it higher than the more publicized Panama Canal of the same period. New York chose this canal instead of a more ambitious ship canal or a small enlargement of the existing canal because the Barge Canal was the most economically feasible way to meet the state's canal transportation needs.

This first battle over, the state and its citizens looked to the next phase—the construction of the Barge Canal.

3 A Canal in the Making

Canal construction in New York State was radically changed in the twentieth century by a new building material. Concrete was liberally used on the Barge Canal—three million cubic yards of it—and this use dramatically distinguishes this canal from its predecessors.[1] The cut-stone masonry of the nineteenth-century Erie Canal differed little in appearance from structures centuries older; when completed, the structures of the Barge Canal were smoother, stronger, and "modern."

Another difference between the building of the Barge Canal and the first Erie came with the first shovel of dirt. When Clinton's Ditch was begun at Rome in 1817, the event was accompanied by a host of dignitaries and ceremonies; the Barge received no documented fanfare when its ground was first broken.

Work began on the new canal system on the Champlain Barge Canal at Fort Miller in April 1905. Dirt was moved on the Erie Barge Canal for the first time at Waterford on June 7, 1905.[2] The entire length of the Erie Barge was open to traffic on May 15, 1918.

New York State would spend as much on this single rebuilding effort as it had on constructing and maintaining all of its nineteenth-century canals. Months of detailed planning were needed; costs and alternatives were always ready to support second guesses of earlier decisions. Additional complexity resulted from the state's relationships with contractors—as it had with its nineteenth-century system, the state hired private contractors. Sections and structures of the canal were divided to enable different companies to bid on the work. This enabled companies to share the potential profit, and it freed the state from having to attract and manage its own army of workers. More than 200 different contracts eventually were awarded for the Barge Canal System—for building machinery, sometimes for digging miles of new canal, sometimes for dredging a canalized river—not including a nearly equal number of contracts for building the canal terminals. Some of these contracts were as small as $6,090 (for building a road bridge over the canal at Little

Opposite:
This construction view looking east from the Lockport locks in 1912 shows the partially completed Barge Canal chamber next to the remaining Enlarged Erie locks. The Barge replaced the southern half of the famous flight of locks, leaving only the north wall of that portion still visible today.   *New York State Archives*

Contractors who built the Barge Canal had to move in or construct large pieces of equipment to do the job. In this 1907 view, men stand on a rail-mounted pile driver at the site of Erie Barge Canal Lock 10 in Cranesville.

New York State Archives

Falls), to over $1 million for Locks 34 and 35 in Lockport. Some of the more unusual contracts were for moving graves from cemeteries in the canal's right-of-way.

Work began almost simultaneously at sites throughout the state. By 1906, contractors were working on a Mohawk River dam and lock, on the northern part of the Champlain Canal, on the eastern end of the Erie Canal at Waterford, on the canal in Little Falls, at the western end of the Erie, and on part of the Oswego Canal through Fulton.

Since much of the work on the canal was in relatively remote areas and went on for many months, contractors built labor camps of shanties and outlying huts. Unskilled laborers lived in the camps (skilled laborers, time keepers, and mechanics usually boarded in nearby cities or farmhouses along the line of the canal) and paid about a dollar per month for their bunks. They shopped at the nearby supply store operated by the labor agent, who managed the camp and made sure that enough labor was available to the contractor. For his trouble, the agent kept the bed fee as well as the profits from the company store.

Some labor agents took their efforts one step further: They charged the men for getting the job, then charged them for the sleeping room whether they used it or not. One inspector observed that this arrangement "is extortion pure and simple; this, together with what is derived from the sale of food and drink, enables the 'padrone' (labor agent) to get about all the money the men spend. Cases are known of one padrone bidding against another by offering to supply all necessary unskilled labor at a lower rate of wages in return for the 'privilege' of the shanty and store." The shanties themselves tended to be simple rooms, poorly ventilated, with bunks—often just board berths filled with straw or hay with an old blanket thrown over them—all around.

Wages varied at the work sites depending on the type of job. The captain of a dredge got $5 per day, a deckhand just $2 per day, a stone mason $4 a day, and a waterboy (who made sure the men were adequately supplied with drinking water) just 91 cents per day.

Like the state's canals before it, construction of the Barge Canal relied on immigrant labor, including Austrians, Hungarians, and a good number of Italians.[3] In one 1908 study, almost half the workers on 21 Barge Canal contracts were not United States citizens.

The 1903 Barge Canal Law allowed the state engineer to appropriate any land that was necessary to build the canal, and the state's Court of Claims determined how much compensation a property owner would get, a process that (naturally) often received complaints. Lawyers tried to convince landowners that they could get the landowners more for the appropriated land— for a 10 percent cut of the award. These "Ten Per Cent Men" were "known up and down the valley and across the State wherever the Barge Canal is being built."[4] In fact, these lawyers sometimes tried to get entire communities to make exclusive

Labor camps such as this one in 1910 near Rome were built along the canal to house canal construction workers.
New York State Archives

One of the first steps in building the Barge Canal was to clear the land. In this 1906 view near Montezuma, timber has been cleared and prepared for burning before digging begins for the new Erie Barge Canal.

New York State Archives

contracts with them to deal with the state. At Northwood, the site of the Hinckley Reservoir, everyone apparently held back from making a deal with the lawyers until the lawyers got one prominent citizen to sign; the entire town then followed suit. One Syracuse law firm held 300 claims but had not settled any by 1913.[5] There were claims for flooded land where reservoirs were built, claims by railroad companies forced to build new crossings over the canal, and claims where industrial buildings were destroyed or relocated. By 1913 there were an estimated $50 million in claims, but, as one paper noted, "it is obvious that the claimants can't have all they are asking."[6]

In 1907, construction continued more ambitiously when more contracts were awarded, including Contract 12 for 49 miles of canal west of Oneida Lake, and Contract 14 for the massive dams at Crescent and Vischer Ferry. Engineers were still working on a number of problems before awarding some contracts—where to site the canal through Rome, how to lessen the chance of flooding from the Genesee River, and what kind of dam to put in the Oswego River at Phoenix to prevent flooding at Syracuse, among many others. Elsewhere, construction equipment was put in place at sites all along the canal so that more substantial progress would be made after the planning and preparation years

A LONG HAUL

Frank Williams, the DeWitt Clinton of the Barge Canal

Frank Williams gave a good share of his professional life to building the Barge Canal—he was state engineer and surveyor for over half of the years of its construction.[7] Noble Whitford, in his classic 1921 history of the Barge Canal, said that "it is he . . . whom history will acclaim the builder of the new waterway; it is he who will be known as the DeWitt Clinton or Colonel Goethals of the Barge canal."[8] Whitford added that the honor was not just because of Williams' many years of service during the canal construction, but because of the monumental problems he resolved.

Frank Williams brought a broad background to the Barge Canal project. Born in 1873 in Durhamville, a bustling Erie Canal town with many impressive canal structures nearby, he attended Colgate University in Hamilton just 12 years after the Chenango Canal through the village had been abandoned. He went on to study law at Syracuse University and graduated in 1897. From college, he went on to a job in the state engineer and surveyor's office as a rodman, working on the ill-fated Nine-Million-Dollar Improvement project. He later worked on Bond's 1901 study that became the blueprint for the Barge Canal. In 1908 he was elected state engineer and surveyor, the first of an unprecedented series of five two-year terms.

As state engineer, he was involved with such important canal issues as the development of the Terminal Act and the construction of the freight houses, grain elevators, and harbors; the addition of the Cayuga and Seneca Canal; establishment of the "blue line" surveys that defined state canal lands; experiments with concrete for canal structures; requesting of additional money to complete the canal; and dealing with uncooperative railroads in establishing crossings.

Even after the canal was completed, Williams was one of its strongest advocates. With the canal in the hands of the federal government during World War I, some observers felt the railroads had put their collective thumb over the Barge Canal and squashed any commercial progress it might have made early on. Williams implored the federal government to return the canal to New York State control. "If we could be relieved of that uncertainty [federal control], it would give us a chance to develop our canal system," he stated.[9] He also lamented the proposal from western states to build a ship canal along the St. Lawrence River—the Barge Canal, Williams' great engineering effort, had only been open two years. He concluded in 1925 that special interests and federal regulations from the war had prevented the canal's commercial success.

In 1922, Frank Williams did not run for another term as state engineer and surveyor because his Republican Party did not choose him for the slate. He went back to private practice and worked on other engineering feats such as the Holland and Lincoln Tunnels in New York City. He died in 1930 at the age of 56. The editor of the *Rome Daily Sentinel* eulogized that "he was steadfast, capable and he demanded good service. He was a young man then—young for such responsibilities. He was not fashioned to swim with the political trickery of the time and he did not do it. He played a fair game with the state and an intellectual game."[10]

of 1905 and 1906. The next two years showed a large increase in construction, even more in the next two years. From 1911 to 1915, over $50 million of work was done, compared to just $1 million in 1905. In those latter four years, the Cayuga and Seneca Canal was added to the work roster, as well as terminal construction at many cities and towns along the route (which had been unplanned in the 1903 authorization).

From February 1908 to January 1919, the state engineer published the *Barge Canal Bulletin*, which included monthly updates and discussions of the issues the builders were facing. Although extensive surveys, maps, plans, and calculations had been completed before the canal bill was adopted, these plans had to be fine tuned before construction could start, including the type of concrete to use, how to design the various dams, and how to assure there would be enough water to maintain the system. The *Bulletin* detailed the struggles and achievements of building the Barge Canal while attempting to prove to New Yorkers that they had invested in something they would be proud of when it was completed.

One of the earliest noteworthy challenges was to design dams that would adapt the Mohawk River for barge navigation. The original plans specified traditional, fixed-wall dams, "the style . . . that has been in use for centuries, which has a crest that cannot be raised or lowered and holds back the water to a minimum level at all times."[11] Engineers recognized a problem with this type of dam: Water could not flow down the river fast enough in times of high water, thus contributing to flooding. A movable dam, on the other hand, could be raised out of the river during the flood season to let the water flow unimpeded. Movable dams, consisting of gate sections that could be lowered into a recess below the river bed, had been used for several decades by the time the Barge was designed.

The engineers saw the movable dam design as a good solution to the Mohawk River problem for a number of reasons. Because the old Erie Canal had gone through the same valley and had brought prosperity and population to the banks of the river, a flood could be devastating in more ways than one—any flooding caused by fixed dams might have made the state liable for damages. With movable dams, the state could claim that such floods were completely an act of nature. Also, the movable dams saved money because they lessened the amount of dredging required. The crest height of a movable dam could be made higher than that of a fixed dam at a given location, since it was removed in flood season (a fixed dam required a greater margin

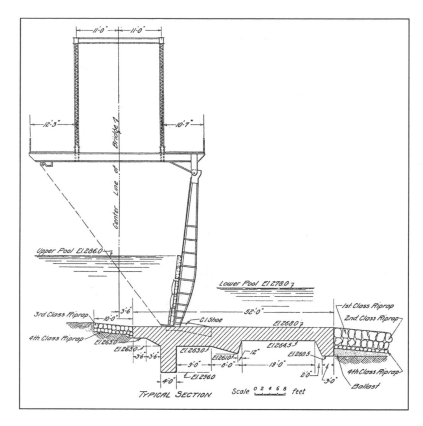

TYPICAL SECTION.   Scale 0 2 4 6 8 feet

This line drawing of the movable dam gate shows how the frame sets into the concrete shoe under the water.

Barge Canal Book of Plans (1920)

of safety to lessen threats of flooding; the extra height of the movable dam meant sufficient water depth could be maintained behind the dam, which meant less dredging was needed). Finally, movable dams would prevent silt from collecting behind them, an inherent problem with fixed dams—silt would be swept away when the dam was raised out of the water each year.[12]

To aid the design of these dams, the engineers studied existing dams in the United States and Europe. A movable dam on the Moldau River (in what is now the Czech Republic) became the model for the Barge's Mohawk dams. The style known as a *bridge dam* with *Boule gates* (steel frames with movable steel plates inside) was adopted because it was the most reliable and easiest to operate. The engineer who eventually drew the plans said his goals were to "reproduce the natural area of discharge at each site, so as to avoid changing flood heights; to use high dams so as to reduce their number and length and, therefore, their cost; to use few pieces so as to concentrate the strength and reduce the number of pieces to be handled; to place a minimum amount of steelwork permanently under water because of rusting; to make all parts of plain workmanship, etc., and similar as far as practicable; and to incorporate only such features as had been successfully adopted elsewhere, or about whose success there appeared to be

The gates of the movable dam at Erie Barge Canal Lock 9 have been pulled out of the water as part of emergency repairs in July 1952 when a portion of the dam failed. The people in the center of the picture are dwarfed by the size of the dam.

Canal Society of New York State
(Gayer Collection)

no reasonable doubt."[13] Since their construction nearly 90 years ago, the dams have indeed proven to be durable and efficient.

The first of the movable dams became operational in 1911. The dam at Fort Plain's Lock 15 received the first of the winches; after installation the gates were lowered into place against the concrete sill at the bottom.[14]

In the land-cut sections, steam shovels did most of the excavation work. The excavated dirt was placed by the shovels onto *dump wagons* (rail-mounted cars on temporary tracks in the bed of the channel); a small steam locomotive pulled the cars out of the channel and brought them back empty (horses and wagons were also used, just as in the construction of earlier canals). An incredible amount of dirt had to be moved, even by today's standards. The progress of the excavation was continually monitored and frequently compared to the construction of the Panama Canal, which was occurring at the same time. In February 1908, a chart in the *Barge Canal Bulletin* showed the two canals excavated about the same amount of material each year.

Some unique machinery was designed to meet the challenging excavation at the Rochester rock cut. One was a *tipple incline*. With cables, cars loaded with five to six cubic yards of rock were pulled out of the bed of the cut. Looking like a steel bridge on an angle, the incline hung over the outside of the prism so that loads

could be dumped onto the gathering piles of rocks that paralleled the outside of the canal channel.

The *grab machine* was another marvel at the Rochester cut. The machine looked like a large steel bridge that stretched well above the canal channel and sides, its 400-foot length long enough to hang beyond the sides of the canal. Two 90-foot towers supported the span and moved it along temporary railroad tracks in the canal bed. In the center of the span was a trolley-like car that traveled to its ends. A mammoth steel grab bucket, looking like a large iron jaw, was attached by cables beneath the car. The bucket was lowered onto and closed around a dozen cubic yards of rock; it was then lifted and

Above:
Top: Much of the excavation for the Barge Canal was done with steam shovels, like this one working on the canal prism west of Oneida Lake in 1908. The dirt and rock was scooped out with the shovel and placed in the dump cars on the right.   *New York State Archives.*
Bottom: Dump wagons were used to remove excavated material out of a work area. This 1906 view shows a spoil bank at Cranesville.

New York State Archives

Above:
Specialized machinery was developed
to excavate the rock cut west of
Rochester. This bridge-like structure,
called the grab machine, supported a
scoop on a long cable and moved along
the channel on rails. Excavated
material was carried to the side of the
prism and unloaded.

New York State Archives

Opposite:
Top: The hydraulic dredge *Ontario,*
working near Weedsport, has its cutter
heads raised out of the water in this
1906 view.   *New York State Archives*
Middle: This ladder dredge is moving
material from the land cut near Brewerton to the side of the canal in 1912. The
dredge's buckets moved along its length
as on a conveyor belt.

New York State Archives
Bottom: The large shovel, or dipper (on
the dipper dredge *Hurricane* in this
picture) is scooping material from the
State Ditch along the Seneca River in
1909.   *New York State Archives*

carried by the car to the side of the canal, where its contents
were dumped into huge piles of rock that remain to this day. A
contemporary observer noted that the grab machine's "lofty and
imposing frame-work, outlined against the sky, is a dominant
feature of the landscape. The curiosity of thousands of passing
travelers by the railway is divided between the bridge conveyor
and its product—the rock piles which it builds."[15]

As the land lines were being excavated, monstrous steam-
powered hulks began appearing in the rivers to dredge the river
bottoms to assure a 12-foot depth for navigation. These dredges
usually carried crews that worked in three 8-hour shifts a day, six
days a week. In 1908, the *Barge Canal Bulletin* termed
"remarkable" the 216,425 cubic yards the dredge *Fort Edward* had
moved in a single month.[16] In 1909 another vessel took 454,706
cubic yards out of the Montezuma marshes. A year later the
record was again broken: The dredge *Champlain* counted
470,352 cubic yards in a single month.[17]

There were three main types of dredges in use on the canal—
hydraulic (suction), dipper (shovel) and ladder (bucket). The
hydraulic dredges worked best at removing sand and fine gravel
(nothing that was too heavy or had big rock in it); they suctioned
material out of the bottom of the river like a vacuum cleaner and
pushed it through a pipeline (supported on pontoons) to a point
on shore called a *spoil bank* or *spoil lagoon,* where the dirt settled

out and the water returned to the river. The hydraulic dredge looked like a rectangular, boxy boat, with the long tail of the pipeline connecting it to the shore.

The *ladder dredge* consisted of a bucket-and-conveyor system. The buckets scooped the material from the river bottom and moved it onto a conveyor. The conveyor was pulled behind the dredge and dropped the material either into a waiting scow or onto shore, depending on how wide the water was at that point.

The *dipper dredge* was simply a steam shovel mounted on a barge: The shovel scooped material from the bottom of the river, swung around, and dropped it in a waiting scow or along shore. All three types of dredges were moved around the canal system as needed, sometimes in pieces to be reassembled at the desired spot.

But canal engineers were concerned not only with digging the canal channel, they also needed to ensure there was enough water to fill it in the spring and to replace any lost from lockages, leaks, and evaporation. There were two critical sections—the western end from Tonawanda to beyond Rochester, and the summit level near Rome. The Rome summit of the nineteenth-century Erie always had challenged engineers, and the Barge builders wanted to be sure the new canal would not run out of water along the same level, so two substantial dams were constructed to assure water for the summit—Delta and Hinckley Dams. The 100-foot-high Delta Dam stops the water of the Mohawk River about five miles north of Rome, forming a reservoir known as Delta Lake. (The village of Delta is now at the bottom of the lake. Before the reservoir was filled, workers removed 295 buildings from the village and realigned a portion of the nearby Black River Canal.) Hinckley Reservoir stores water from West Canada Creek about 20 miles north of Utica. Water released beyond its 82-foot-high dam flows in the West Canada Creek bed for five miles. At that point, some water is diverted to Nine Mile Creek via a nearly six-mile-long artificial channel; Nine Mile Creek empties into the Barge Canal opposite Oriskany.

Both these northern reservoirs tap watersheds that include portions of the Adirondacks. The diversion of water for Delta is still aided by a mid-nineteenth-century feeder and reservoir system designed for the Black River Canal and earlier Erie Canal.

Similarly, south of Rome, several other nineteenth-century reservoirs continue in service for the Barge. Water from Jamesville, DeRuyter, and Erieville Reservoirs enters the Barge Canal at New London via a portion of the Enlarged Erie Canal, now the Old Erie Canal State Park. Reservoirs that were

established near Hamilton for the Chenango Canal in the 1830s provide water east of the Rome summit after emptying their waters into Oriskany Creek.

The western section of the canal presented its own unique water problems. One engineer stated that "the greatest independent water supply required for the Erie Canal at any point is that necessary for the western section."[18] The canal builders, however, knew that the Niagara River and its connection to Lake Erie would be sufficient for this section if only the water could be uniformly distributed eastward. A slight slope was designed into the canal bottom on the long western levels so that Niagara River water could float boats to well east of Rochester.

Water for the summit of the Champlain Barge Canal comes from the improved nineteenth-century Glens Falls Feeder. This 12-mile-long feeder diverts water from the Hudson River at Glens Falls and delivers it to the summit level near Fort Edward.

Sufficient water was a critical requirement for the operation of the enlarged locks on the new canal. When first designed, the locks of the Barge Canal were large enough to permit 1,000-ton barges to pass—the 1903 Barge Canal Law allowed for locks 328 feet long but only 28 feet wide (while the lock width on

Although construction progress was made rapidly, there were some setbacks, such as this July 1916 view of the flood-damaged powerhouse at Lock 29 in Palmyra. This powerhouse was destroyed and a new one built.

New York State Archives

contemporary Canadian canals, such as the Welland, was 45 feet). New York City shippers requested the Barge locks to be larger because they expected the two systems to exchange commerce. Before any locks were actually built, state officials agreed to increase the width to 45 feet.

Some smaller locks were built to link the Barge Canal to portions of the nineteenth-century canals that would still be used, if only temporarily. For instance, before the new Barge channel south of Rochester was completed, a junction lock allowed older, smaller boats to lock into the old section of the Erie and go around the new, uncompleted section. Junction locks at New London on the Erie, and at Fort Edward and Schuylerville on the Champlain, continued to provide access to sections of the old canals well after the 1918 completion of the Barge. The Schuylerville lock was used until the 1950s, making it the last operating junction lock. The New London lock was rebuilt in the 1920s to serve as a dry dock for boat repairs and continues to be used as such. Other shorter-lived examples of junction locks include one at Rome, where a junction lock connected the Barge with a short stretch of the old Erie so that the Black River Canal could continue to be used. Similar locks at Mohawk and on the

Lock construction made liberal use of concrete with complex systems to get the concrete to the walls and floors that needed it. This 1908 view shows Lock 5 at Waterford in progress, with wooden framing still attached.

New York State Archives

A LONG HAUL

south side of the Barge at Rome kept open the old canal through Utica until local residents forced its closure in the early 1920s.

The walls and floors of the regular Barge Canal lift locks were made of concrete unless the lock rested on rock (such as at Erie Barge Lock 17 in Little Falls, where the standard concrete floor was not needed). The walls were built in a stepped fashion: The top of the wall is 5 to 12 feet thick while the base is 13 to 34 feet thick. Underneath each lock (unless it's built on rock), pilings were pushed into the ground to give a stable foundation. Within the walls, culverts or long tunnels the length of the lock carry the water that enters and leaves the lock chamber. The valves that control the water flow within these tunnels are powered by a 3- or 7-horsepower motor, depending on the size of the tunnel—the larger lift locks have 7- by 9-foot tunnels, while the smaller ones have 5- by 7-foot tunnels. In some of the locks, another culvert was positioned alongside to supply water for the hydroelectric powerhouses. A turbine driven by this water originally produced the primary power for lights at the locks and to run the machinery needed to open and close the gates.

At first glance, the lock gates seem to be made only of steel. However, the vertical quoin post at the gate hinge and the toe

The Barge Canal made liberal use of concrete instead of the cut stone of the earlier canals, which created smooth, modern-looking structures. This 1910 view of Champlain Barge Lock 8 in Fort Edward shows the lock almost complete, waiting to be back filled.
New York State Archives

post at the seam between the two gates are made of white oak. The cushioning of the wood forms a more water-tight seal than steel alone would. The gates operate on a seven-horsepower motor and are designed to open and close in about a minute.

The Barge Canal locks were all fitted with *buffer beams* to protect the gates from being rammed by an out-of-control vessel. (This safety feature was partly inspired by a 1909 accident on a Canadian canal, where a boat outside a lock crashed into the lower gates, causing substantial damage to the lock and to other boats.) The buffer beam was a steel arm outside of the lock chamber designed to swing out from a recess in the concrete approach wall, across the channel to a notch on the other side. A boat would hit the 45-foot-long beam before it struck the lock gates, slowing (if not stopping) it.

Though well meaning, the buffer beams apparently were never used for their intended purpose. Indeed, they may have never even been hooked up to the control panel of the lock, many of

An Unusual Numbering System

There are a number of unexpected sequences in the numbering of the locks on the Barge Canal System. Some numbers are apparently missing; others appear to be later additions. Some locks never received formal numbers. (The junction lock to Utica harbor is an example of this omission, as are the east and west guard locks that protect the Genesee River crossing. The latter, in fact, barely count, since the river's fluctuations are now calmed by the 1951 Mount Morris Dam.)

On the Champlain Barge Canal, there is no Lock 10. Although its construction just north of Smith's Basin was contemplated in a 1906 contract, it was never built. Its proposed eight-foot lift was later incorporated into Lock 9 and other adjustments. (A more creative explanation for the disappearance of Lock 10 comes from Ralph Folger, former canal floating plant supervisor for the New York State Department of Transportation. He "and others have heard, though they never actually saw it happen, that Lock 10 was brought to the 1939 New York World's Fair as part of the State's exhibit. The State apparently forgot to bring it back.")[19]

On the Oswego Canal, Lock 4 was eliminated when engineers determined that Locks 3 and 5 could be deepened and the expensive construction of Lock 4 avoided. Also, a factory adjacent to a dam at the proposed site of Lock 4 was bought by the state and the dam was then removed, along with the need for a lock.

The Erie Canal begins its numbering with Lock 2 in Waterford. What happened to Lock 1? The Barge Canal planners decided that Lock 1 for the Erie Barge Canal would be the Hudson River lock, an updated replacement of the state's nineteenth-century Troy "sloop" lock. The federal government eventually agreed to construct the lock and its associated channel in the Hudson, so the state's Barge Canal does not officially begin until Waterford. (The state did not number the federally operated locks and dam as part of its system.) Similarly, another federal lock controls the western end of the Erie Barge Canal. This Black Rock lock also lacks a state-designated number to mark its position as the next lock west of Lock 35 at Lockport.

There is no Erie Barge Lock 31. Its omission is related to the modified numbering implied by Wayne County Locks 28A and 28B. The chief reason for the unusual numbering there was a last-minute change in the route: A 1910 map of the canal while it was under construction shows Locks 27 and 28 in Lyons, no lock at Newark, and Locks 29 and 30 at Palmyra. Eventually, a lock was built in Newark (28B) and only one at Palmyra (29). The canal engineers had changed their minds about where the canal should go, opting for an alternative path between Lyons and Palmyra. To avoid confusion with the earlier designs, the old numbers were abandoned. While the original numbers were used for unchanged locks, the newly designed ones required new numbers; the designations "A" and "B" resulted. Lock 31 was no longer needed.[20]

which still bear the "Buffer Beam" position. The beams were used for many years to support coffer dams at those locks that needed to be emptied for winter maintenance, though today even that use has ceased. They have been replaced by large steel beams that frequently rest alongside the lock; a crane can position the new beam to support a coffer dam in rebuilt notches in the concrete walls.

The first lock to open on the Barge Canal was Erie Barge Lock 24 in Baldwinsville. On May 9, 1910, the lock was used to pass the state dredge, with its accompanying houseboat and scows. Since gate-operating machinery was not yet installed, a horse was used to open the gates and chain hoists were used to open the valves. According to an observer, they "worked somewhat stiffly, but the lock chamber filled smoothly and it appears that its operation will be satisfactory after a little wear has adjusted the several parts."[21]

At most locks, tall, boxy concrete buildings were erected to shelter the machinery needed to generate power for the locks. Canal historian and engineer Noble Whitford observed that "often it is necessary to pass water around a lock to supply the needs of the lower levels and in such instance power goes to waste unless there is present a plant to develop it. Also the cost of installing a plant at a lock is confined chiefly to the machinery, since conduits and wheel-pits may be formed simply by leaving cavities in the lock walls. Moreover, the locks of today are too large to be operated by hand and thus it is that we find power-plants on all modern canals."[22] Powerhouses were white, concrete buildings, 20 by 30 feet by 20 feet high, with dark-green tile roofs.[23] Forty-three power houses and three substations provided power for the 58 locks on the system. Each power station had two turbines producing 250 volts DC. Sometimes power from one lock's station was used to power a nearby lock, such as Erie Lock 33 did for Lock 32 in Pittsford, at Erie Locks 21 and 22 in New London, and Champlain Locks 7 and 8 in Fort Edward. (Between the Pittsford locks the original concrete poles that carried the electrical lines between the locks can still be seen.) Horizontal-shaft generators were used at the five locks where there was not sufficient drop to power a traditional, vertical-shaft system—Erie Barge Canal Lock 23 near Brewerton is an example of the former. These generators look like huge coffee cans on their sides, as compared to the vertical-shaft generators, which look like cones.

At some locks (generally those located alongside the Mohawk movable dams), water-powered generators were impractical since electricity could not be generated when the dams were raised for the winter. Each of these locks received a pair of gasoline engines that powered the generators—they supplied enough power to operate the gates on the dam, the lock, and 12 arc lamps used along the approach walls.

This power self-sufficiency was important because, at the time, there were no large-scale commercial electrical grids. Once electricity became commercially available the locks were gradually connected over a period of decades; today, all the locks are linked to outside power sources. Where they survive, the original generators are maintained as emergency backups—a few of the hydroelectric powerhouses thus remain in beautifully preserved operating condition. Lock 5 on the Champlain Canal, along with Locks 23 and 28B on the Erie, and Lock 4 on the Cayuga and Seneca, are excellent examples.

Early on, engineers were confronted with challenges that went beyond construction problems or the immediate interests of the canal. For instance, although they had planned to take the canal right through Rome, some citizens there were not keen on the idea—they already disliked the inconveniences the current canal brought into their increasingly congested urban environment. The long approaches for bridges over the canal would get only worse with the Barge. There also was the problem of where to cross the New York Central rail line at Rome and of how to relocate the line. In response, the canal eventually was located just south of the city.[24]

At Rochester, engineers needed a design that would avoid adding to the potential flooding of the Genesee River in the city and yet provide enough deep water to allow boats to cross the river.[25] The movable gates of the Court Street Dam provided this capability as well as a navigable spur into downtown.

Syracuse posed a similar problem. Unlike its nineteenth-century predecessor, the new canal avoided the city entirely. Following the Oneida and Seneca Rivers, the route went well north of the city. In order to allow city businesses and industries to reach the canal, a provision was included in the Barge Canal legislation that required the outlet for Onondaga Lake into the Seneca River be enlarged to accommodate canal boats. Once boats reached the lake, the channel was to be maintained deep enough for boats to reach the head of the lake and into Syracuse, where a harbor was built. This access to the Barge Canal at Syracuse continues to be used today.

In 1907, the state superintendent of public works said that the new construction was making it difficult to keep the old canals open during the navigation season, particularly on the Oswego

Barge Canal. Beginning in 1909, portions of the old Oswego were closed for six seasons as the new canal was being built.[26]

During the winter of 1908 to 1909, more than 40 culverts on the old Erie between Rochester and Lockport were lengthened for Barge Canal use. The superintendent was skeptical about this reuse—a cheaper alternative to totally new construction—and he expected leaks in these already half-century-old structures when the canal was refilled in the spring. Patrols kept a constant watch for failure; a temporary telephone line was installed to speed word of a leak and materials were stored for making emergency repairs. Sure enough, leaks appeared in over a dozen of the hybrid structures before the canal was even filled. The canal had to be drained and new concrete linings added to these troublesome culverts.[27]

While all of this construction was going on, many talked about adding to the not-yet-completed canal. The improvement of the Cayuga and Seneca Canal to Barge Canal standards was added to the construction plan in 1909 at a projected cost of $8 million. (Originally, the existing nineteenth-century Cayuga and Seneca was to remain as a navigable feeder, like the Black River Canal in Rome. Supporters of the improvement recognized the chance to add about 80 miles of natural navigation through two lakes.

The culvert in Medina, the only Erie Canal culvert for a roadway, was rebuilt for the Barge Canal. The facing stones seen in this 1905 view were removed when the culvert was lengthened for the Barge Canal. The stone was numbered and then replaced so that today the structure looks similar to the way it looked in 1905.

New York State Archives

The combination locks (Locks 2 and 3) on the Cayuga and Seneca Barge Canal replaced four Cayuga and Seneca Canal locks in the village of Seneca Falls and radically changed the look of the village. This aerial view of the locks and dam shows Van Cleef Lake in the foreground, which formed when the locks were built. The lake covered a good share of the industrial section of Seneca Falls and the old Cayuga and Seneca Canal.

New York State Electric and Gas

Cement and salt, bulk-loaded products that were ideal for the new Barge Canal, were still important lake-front industries.)

The new Cayuga and Seneca Barge Canal replaced the 11 locks of the older canal with just four. Locks 2 and 3 are in combination at Seneca Falls. Their position east of the village drastically changed the look of Seneca Falls. Van Cleef Lake was formed west of the locks, covering up much of the historic industrial center of the community—in fact, the "falls" of Seneca Falls. About 60 houses of the residential community at "The Flats" were demolished or removed before the mile-long, thousand-foot-wide lake was formed. One hundred sixteen businesses were similarly treated, including the ancestral buildings of today's Gould Pump and the American-LaFrance Company (of fire engine fame). The former received perhaps the single largest cash settlement for damages to property resulting from the Barge's construction; the latter never resumed operations in Seneca Falls. Even the Trinity Episcopal Church, an imposing stone building on the edge of the lake, lost its basement to the canal. To quote a resident at the time, "The Barge Canal gave us a beautiful village, but, oh what a price we paid."[28]

In 1912 a spectacular break occurred in the canal just east of Rochester on the Irondequoit embankment. There, between 1911 and 1912 a pile of dirt over 50 feet high and about three miles long was formed to fill a valley; a concrete trough was laid on top of the embankment to form the canal. A concrete culvert underneath the embankment allowed the Irondequoit Creek to flow under the canal. After the construction was completed in April 1912, water was let into the trough and boats began to use the new crossing. All was going well until later that fall: Apparently, water had been leaking through the trough into the culvert below. The culvert weakened and fell in on September 6, taking the embankment and trough with it in a spectacular collapse that created a gap all the way to the valley floor.[29] Because the failure occurred during the height of the grain-shipping season, "temporary repairs were rushed through by emergency crews working night and day. The mule teams of many of the delayed canal boats were put to work hauling dirt to build up the embankment."[30]

The quick fix involved building a wooden flume on piles driven into the valley floor. The flume connected the two sides of the break so that one lane of canal traffic could cross. A

The Irondequoit Creek Embankment east of Rochester was a great engineering effort—and also the site of a great disaster. Shortly after the long concrete flume high above the valley floor was filled with water, the embankment broke and the water from the canal went cascading down the valley. To keep navigation going while the break was being repaired, a wooden one-lane channel was erected over the break. This 1913 view shows the high embankment and the temporary channel. The embankment of the Enlarged Erie Canal veers off to the right of the picture. *New York State Archives*

Canal Terminals

Public docking was provided by the state at the following locations under the Terminal Act of 1911. Sometimes just a vertical wall at which vessels could tie up sufficed; other sites involved extensive buildings and equipment for loading, unloading, and storing goods. Many of the properties remain in public hands.

Buffalo (Ohio Basin)	Fort Plain
Buffalo (Erie Basin)	Canajoharie
Tonawanda	Fonda
N. Tonawanda	Amsterdam
Lockport (Upper Terminal)	Schenectady
Lockport (Lower Terminal)	Crescent
Middleport	Cohoes
Medina	Troy (Upper Terminal)
Albion	Troy (Lower Terminal)
Holley	Albany
Brockport	Mechanicville
Spencerport	Schuylerville
Rochester	Thomson
Newark	Fort Edward
Lyons	Whitehall
Ithaca	Port Henry
Weedsport	Plattsburgh
Syracuse	Rouses Point
Oswego (River Terminal)	New York City (W. 53rd St.)
Oswego (Lake Terminal)	New York City (East River/ Pier 5)
Constantia	New York City (East River/ Pier 6)
Cleveland	
Rome	Gowanus Bay
Utica	Greenpoint
Frankfort	Long Island City
Ilion	
Herkimer	Hallets Cove
Little Falls	Mott Haven
Saint Johnsville	Flushing

The following additional sites were built as part of the original plans for the Barge Canal and were later considered terminals.[34]

Pittsford	Baldwinsville
Fairport	Fulton
Palmyra	Brewerton
Seneca Falls	Waterford

permanent repair was not completed until the spring of 1918. (Evidence of the temporary wooden trough can still be seen today where the concrete on the south wall juts out around the ghost of the trough.)

Another change in construction plans that had more far-reaching implications occurred in 1912. Several years earlier the state had realized that intrastate use of the canal system required guaranteed public access to the waterway for the transfer of goods from barges to shore. Already, competitors (such as the railroads) had locked up some prime canal frontage. Because it would build them, the state hoped the operation of the shipping terminals would not be influenced by private commercial interests, allowing access to all. (That the issue of terminals had not come up earlier was probably due to the belief that the canal would be principally for through-state products, such as grain, with little need for terminals except at the ends.) The piers, basins, harbors, and docks of the terminals became an important part of the canal because they allowed access. One writer at the time said that "waterways without terminals are like electric wires without contacts."[31] Terminals provided unloading machinery, a public place to store freight until it could be picked up, and a place for boats to dock. A few terminals enhanced their commercial use by developing rail connections.

Commercial use of the terminals never matched expectations. As early as 1924 a state official remarked that "the State has wasted thousands of dollars in the construction of terminals which have never been used and the installation of terminal appliances which have never handled a pound of freight." He concluded that the terminals resulted from "the best example of wasteful legislation that can be found on the statute books of the State."[32] Some of the terminals were soon incorporated into the state's maintenance facilities and abandoned any pretense of commercial use. Canal shops today in Herkimer, Utica, Syracuse, and Albion continue to use these sites and their old freight houses. The remaining terminals resumed their historic role of providing public access to the waterway. The 1995 Canal Recreationway Plan identified this access potential as it searched for avenues to channel recreational use onto the system. The reuse of the old freight house and terminal at Ilion in the early 1960s was a harbinger of this increased public access; the 1997 rebuilding of the Frankfort Terminal in cooperation with a charter boat company is a more recent example.

Almost $20 million was spent to build the original 56 terminals.[33] Each was customized to the amount of projected traffic. There were "terminals of various kinds, all the way from the elaborate creations in New York Harbor, where immense sheds on long piers are crowded daily with goods which are handled by the latest type of electrically-operated device or even where a two-million-bushel grain elevator with all its intricate parts is being erected, to the simple structure of some small hamlet, where the whole equipment consists of nothing more than a wall at which boats may land, a leveled area back of it and a humble frame storehouse, and even the storehouse may be lacking."[35] Because dock walls were built for general Barge Canal construction, eight more locations are considered to have terminal facilities though they were not paid for by the Terminal Act; therefore, the actual total number of terminals constructed was 64, and "few towns of size along the canal are without some terminal facilities."[36]

Architectural clues of these public commercial ports can still be seen. Some of the New York City facilities still stand, and the Skenesborough Museum in Whitehall occupies that community's 1918 freight house, a sibling structure of one that once stood in Albany. Similarly large or larger freight houses were built in Buffalo and New York City. The much smaller,

This imposing canal terminal, seen in a 1922 view, was located at Pier 6 on the East River in New York City. The large amount of canal traffic in the city and its exchange with ocean freighters demanded a large terminal such as this. There were only a handful of terminals with this design.   *New York State Archives*

wooden freight houses, with their functional cookie-cutter design, provided more than just a temporary cover to goods traveling on the canal. From Gowanus Bay in Brooklyn to Herkimer to Erie Basin in Buffalo, there were more than 30 of these small structures. Only about a half dozen remain, though even these add to the visual unity to the system.

Along with terminals, the state realized how important grain elevators would be to the commercial viability of the system. Like the public terminals, publicly owned grain elevators were important to haulers as places to store grain. The state already had made provision at the terminals for handling most types of freight, but grain had its own unique requirements. Without grain elevators (especially in New York City), barges would have to wait for ships to arrive before they could unload, tying up a boat that could be back on the canal. Buffalo had a legendary forest of privately operated grain elevators to hold grain from Great Lakes vessels for later shipment on the canal. Along the Barge Canal the state built elevators at Oswego and New York City; public money later helped build grain-storage facilities at Albany. The location of these facilities was based on the flow of grain from large producing areas to consuming areas—placement attempted to equalize supply and demand by storing grain when it was ready to be shipped from the West, even when there was no immediate need for it in the East or Europe, or any means of getting it there. The state's willingness to construct these facilities was another demonstration of the progressive spirit of some early twentieth-century public officials.

The still-standing Oswego grain elevator was built to tap into the grain trade using Lake Ontario instead of the western section of the Barge Canal. Canada tried to secure that trade by enlarging its Welland Canal so that Great Lakes freighters could go from Lake Erie to Lake Ontario, bypassing Buffalo and the Erie Barge Canal entirely; grain elevators at Montreal were the hoped-for destination.[37] New York officials thought that Oswego could be competitive as a port for grain because vessels could carry cargo such as coal from Oswego back through the lakes, whereas Montreal had nothing to offer a return trip.[38]

The Oswego elevator was built in two phases. In 1920, money was appropriated just for the foundation (because the enlarged Welland Canal was still under construction and it was felt that there would not be much grain traffic on the lake until it was finished).[39] The elevator, with a total capacity of one million bushels and consisting of 27 concrete storage bins or silos (each 20 feet in diameter and 94 feet high), was completed in 1924.

Each bin could store the annual production of a hundred average farms.[40] Two large, rail-mounted towers on the lake side of the elevator were used to unload lake freighters. On the other side of the elevator three spouts were used to load canal barges.

The elevator did not see much use until 1932, when the superintendent of public works reported that "for the first time in its history, there has been some real business done at the Oswego grain elevator, and it is hoped that during 1933 sufficient revenue will be received at this elevator to at least cover its operating costs."[41] The complex was transferred in 1958 to the newly created Port of Oswego; it is now little used and its future is uncertain. The H. Lee White Maritime Museum occupies the building that housed the administrative offices and repair shops of the elevator.

The largest of the Barge Canal-era elevators, completed in 1932 in Albany, is operated by Cargill, Inc. It was built as part of the Port of Albany, itself a product of the 1920s deepening of the Hudson River to Albany that allowed ocean-going ships to reach the city. The 13.5-million-bushel elevator is still in use, although the grain is now brought in by railroad.[42]

Another adjunct to the Barge Canal was the system of buoys and other navigation aids. Three-quarters of this new canal comprised lakes and rivers where a comparatively narrow section of water was sufficiently deep—boats had to know where the

The Oswego grain elevator stored one million bushels of grain. Each of the round silos stored the annual production of 100 farms. In this 1937 view (looking northeast), railroad cars are waiting to load on the left side of the elevator. The white building attached to the elevator was the administrative offices and repair shop for the elevator; now it is the home of the H. Lee White Maritime Museum.
New York State Archives

deep channel was. Lighthouses were built on Oneida Lake—at Verona Beach at the eastern end, at Brewerton at the western end, and on Frenchman's Island. The lighthouses are standing today, their lights still operating, though the service they provide is not nearly as vital as it once was. In the 1920s, the treacherous 20-mile lake tossed the boxy wooden barges around when storms came up suddenly, and the lighthouses provided a path to safety for the tugs and barges. They also kept the boats on course when crossing the lake, even on calm days. The three lighthouses have the same design, built of reinforced concrete. A square base provides space for fuel storage and an entry; at the top of the 80-foot tower a large lantern is surrounded by an iron lattice railing, and narrow, rectangular windows are evenly spaced in the tower to provide light inside. The lighthouses now use electric lights.

Piece by piece, like a well-planned jigsaw puzzle, the state's new canal system became operational. In May 1915, a gala celebration on the few but important miles of Barge Canal from Waterford to Rexford marked the opening of that section. The celebration began at Waterford, where the citizens turned out to greet Governor Charles Whitman, State Engineer Frank Williams, Superintendent of Public Works William Wotherspoon, and other state officials. A number of state legislators also were able to attend the celebration because it was so close to Albany. Church bells pealed and fire sirens sounded through the village as the crowds of spectators lined the canal banks and bridges and followed the officials as they locked through the Waterford flight on the *Frisbee*.

After passing through the two guard gates at the upper end of the flight, Governor Whitman formally opened this eastern leg of the Barge Canal and christened Crescent Lake (actually a widened portion of the Mohawk River created by the new Crescent Dam). The public relations effort was certainly successful: Later that year the state engineer asked the citizens of New York for an additional $27 million to finish the Barge Canal. The voters approved the money and the canal flowed on to completion.

On May 15, 1918, in the midst of wartime, the Barge Canal was finally opened end to end. The last barrier was removed on the west bank of the Genesee River south of Rochester. "A modest ceremony had been arranged and a small company composed of members of the engineering staff and a few contractors had gathered to witness the event. The State Engineer, with a shovel taken from one of the laborers, opened a small ditch across the intervening dike, letting the waters of the Genesee through to the new channel. Then an excavating

Three identical lighthouses, 80 feet high, were built to guide canal boats across the sometimes-treacherous 20 miles of Oneida Lake. They are located at Verona Beach, Frenchman's Island and Brewerton. *Drawing by Linda DeVona*

machine with its great bucket scooped out a few yards more and the waters rushed over the barrier. Soon they had torn a large hole in the dike, through which they continued to pour till the channel had been filled."[43]

Thus, the Barge Canal was opened after nearly 15 years of construction. Not, as with the original Erie, with a large group of boats carrying dignitaries and a barrel of water from Lake Erie, not to the sound of cannon fire along the whole route, and not to the sight of fireworks over New York harbor. The new canal was just a sound business investment, an improvement to the celebrated Erie. Quietly, on May 19, 1918, the Rochester *Democrat and Chronicle* mentioned that the "first boat on the Barge Canal to reach Rochester docked at the bridge in Genesee Park last evening. The boat is a steam tug, the 'William D. Kroop' of Buffalo and is on the way to meet a fleet of barges that is coming up from New York."[44] The *Knickerbocker Press* in Albany summarized the broader benefit of the canal's opening on July 4, the day the official celebration took place: "With the adjustment of freight rates, the volume of business that can be diverted from the railroads will relieve greatly the transportation difficulties which have been so acute during the past two years, and open a way for the outlet of shipments direct without charge from the great territories of the west and northwest to tidewater."[45]

There was an official celebration to open the Waterford to Rexford section of the Barge Canal in 1915. Crowds gathered and church bells rang as the official boat carrying Governor Whitman, State Engineer Frank Williams and other officials made its way up the flight. This is a view of the group entering Erie Lock 2.

Canal Society of New York State

4   A Truly Amazing Construction

The construction of the Barge Canal quietly set a number of engineering benchmarks. Recognition of the importance of the new canal was very localized—people were most concerned with the personal inconveniences it caused—yet the mighty water highway surpassed even the Panama Canal's achievements. The Barge was much longer, included many more structures, went through well-developed territory, and had to maintain established canal traffic during construction. A visiting federal engineer was thrilled to be shown all the accomplishments, stating "I can say without reservation that in no other area of the same extent in the world, including the Panama Canal, can an engineer find so much of interest and instructive value in the matter of various types of canalization work. It surprises one after such an inspection that there is not a more general knowledge throughout the country of the canal, its construction and commercial probabilities."[1]

There are specific sites where noteworthy engineering feats deserve special attention.

ERIE LOCKS 34 AND 35 AT LOCKPORT

The vertical drop at Niagara Falls is mirrored at Lockport, where Erie Locks 34 and 35 replaced the flight of five locks needed to climb the Niagara Escarpment on the earlier canals. Also, one set of these five locks was removed. Combining locks like this was common on the state's nineteenth-century canals, but it is rare on the Barge Canal—tandem Locks 34 and 35 are the only combined locks besides Locks 2 and 3 on the Cayuga and Seneca Canal near Seneca Falls.

The tandem locks at Lockport lift boats 49 feet. The upper gates of Lock 35 hold back the water at a navigable level all the way west to the Niagara River. For that reason, there are two sets of upper gates at Lock 35 instead of one in order to provide extra insurance against an accident that might allow Lake Erie to flow

Opposite:
The highest lock on the Barge Canal is Lock 17 at Little Falls. Boats are raised 40.5 feet. The lock has changed from this 1921 view. There is no longer a side pool to recycle water from the lock.

New York State Archives

Above:
This 1918 view of Lockport shows some of the five combined Enlarged Erie Canal locks on the right, the two Barge Canal locks on the left, and the Barge Canal powerhouse in the middle. Factories took advantage of water running through tunnels alongside the locks to power machines.

Canal Society of New York State

Right:
Lock 35 in Lockport has two sets of upper gates because it is the last lock before Lake Erie. The extra set of lock gates seen in this 1921 view (and still there today) is a safeguard.

New York State Archives

uncontrolled into the canal. The protection is supplemented with a guard gate in Pendleton, farther west.

Since Lake Erie provides nearly all the water for the western part of the canal, a continual flow of water needs to pass through the Lockport locks east toward Rochester. A tunnel alongside the locks assists this flow, and also is used for commercial power generation. (The now-gone generators once supplied power for the two locks and the two nearby lift bridges.) Enterprising business people in the 1820s used the canal water that went around the locks of the original canal to run their machinery; indeed, Lockport grew up around the Erie Canal locks to take advantage of the water power. The Barge Canal powerhouse still stands as a small canal museum.

The Barge Canal uses the remaining north set of the five locks to allow water to bypass Locks 34 and 35, offering a useful comparison between the old, small locks and their much larger twentieth-century descendants.

AQUEDUCT AT MEDINA

Continuing east, Oak Orchard Creek, which crosses the canal line near Medina, posed an interesting problem. The old Enlarged Erie Canal followed a tight curve at this point—too sharp for the barges of the new canal to navigate. If the Barge Canal crossed the creek in a straight line it would mean crossing a 500-foot-long, 90-foot-deep gorge. The engineers pondered seven options for the crossing, from a long steel bridge to a huge embankment of dirt with a concrete trough on top (as was constructed at Irondequoit). They chose a concrete arch spanning 300 feet, with a concrete trough to carry the channel. Though later reduced to a 50-foot span, the proposal stretched the known limits of concrete's strength.[2] A number of well-documented tests were performed until the engineers were confident they had formulated concrete that was strong enough. Steel plates were placed in the concrete joints of the trough to inhibit leaks. The canal channel is 125 feet wide as it crosses downtown Medina, 45 feet above the bed of the Oak Orchard Creek gorge.

A huge amount of concrete was needed to build the Medina Aqueduct. This 1922 view shows the arched opening for Oak Orchard Creek at the bottom of the concrete wall. The design of the new arch is a mirror of the previous aqueduct from the Enlarged Erie in that location.   *New York State Archives*

This 1913 view of building the Medina aqueduct shows the sloping outside wall on the right and the prism cut through the dirt on the left.

New York State Archives

After many months of designing and testing, the Barge aqueduct had to be built quickly in order not to interrupt navigation, so as soon as the 1913 navigation season came to an end, work began. The old Enlarged Erie aqueduct was removed first, but not before forms for its concrete replacement were built within its single arch. Always fearing that winter conditions would prevent them from pouring the concrete, the contractor pushed construction through so that the new aqueduct was ready for the opening of the canal in 1914.[3]

Today, the span seems unimpressive—all that can be seen are long stretches of dam-like retaining wall with portions extending to the bottom of the gorge.

THE DEEP CUT AT ROCHESTER

Contract 6 to dig through the rock south of Rochester was let in 1905, among the first for the new canal. The engineers knew this would be a tough section to build—their challenge was to remove 1.5 million cubic yards of rock—and they knew the contract would be costly. The test was to see if their estimates for this section (and by implication for the whole canal) were on target.

The work on the Rochester cut was referred to locally as the "rock piles." Because the Barge skirted south of the original Erie's route through downtown Rochester, Contract 6 was entirely new construction, not an enlargement of the old channel. For 2.5 miles, heavy rock needed to be cut down from 12 to 36 feet, with a width of 94 feet at the bottom. The cut was so deep that excavated rock had to be handled twice to remove it—first it was thrown into the center of the cut by hand or steam shovel, then it was lifted out of the canal channel. Drills and dynamite were used to loosen the material; the unique machinery that was developed for this section—the grab machine and the bridge conveyor to carry the rock out of the deep prism—were described in Chapter 3.

The Rochester cut was completed in 1910, shortly after the death of the contractor, Frank Maselli, the innovator who developed the grab machine. He successfully bid on the job for just over $1 million—$375,690 less than the engineers' estimate.

CHANGING THE CANAL ROUTE IN ROCHESTER

A short distance away from this early work on Rochester's deep cut was a section that was among the very last undertaken, a delay created by engineering and political factors.[4] Local

In 1916, work was still being done on the deep cut west of Rochester. With a 1905 contract, this section was one of the first let. Workers are drilling along the rock face in this view. Housing for the workers is on the bank above.

New York State Archives

residents and state officials concurred that improving the canal along its nineteenth-century route through the congested downtown area was unfeasible, but the city still wanted close connection to the new canal for its business interests. So the new channel was routed south of the city to avoid disruption, though this solution, too, posed problems: The canal would have to cut through one of the city's grandest parks, run along a river notorious for flooding, require six railroad crossings, and compete with rail lines immediately along the river's banks. According to Noble Whitford, "When State Engineer Williams assumed office in 1915, he perceived that the Rochester problem had to be solved speedily or it would block the whole canal scheme. If construction had been begun earlier in this vicinity, doubtless the whole canal could have been opened earlier, or at least it could have been opened without such almost superhuman efforts as were actually required for the accomplishment."[5]

To fit the canal through Rochester's Genesee Valley Park, the engineers decided to build a highway bridge and three ornamental foot bridges that they felt would "harmonize with their surroundings . . . and . . . preserve the beauty of the park."[6] The park had been designed by the famous landscape architect Frederick Law Olmstead at the end of the nineteenth century and it needed to be preserved as much as possible.

Whereas the original canal had crossed the Genesee River on an aqueduct upstream, the Barge would cross the river in a slackwater pool. The Court Street Dam was raised well north of the crossing, in the heart of downtown and not far from the nineteenth-century aqueduct, to create the needed and consistent

When the canal was proposed, Rochester residents were concerned that the canal would affect the beauty of Genesee Valley Park, designed by Frederick Law Olmstead. Three ornamental foot bridges, seen in this 1921 view, were built across the canal at this spot to harmonize the canal with the park surroundings.

New York State Archives

A LONG HAUL

depth for navigation. It was initially built with two movable vertical gates and a section of movable dam (similar to the Mohawk River dams). By 1926, the movable dam was removed so that all of the dam consisted of *sector gates* (adjustable steel gates that look like wedges and allow water to flow over their crests).[7] This new design made the regulation of the river for commercial power generation easier. The local utility company altered the state's dam at its own expense in order to increase its generating potential.

Canal engineers also had to resolve flooding problems caused by the Genesee River's low banks, so the river channel was deepened and concrete retaining walls—higher than were actually needed at the time—were built on each side of the river to protect property from high water. The railroad tracks of the Erie and the Lehigh Valley Railroads were moved to create a new canal harbor for Rochester. A new rail station also was constructed, as were railroad bridges over the canal.

These efforts in Rochester were begun in earnest in 1917; the goal was to open the canal the following year. Completion of the main line of the canal, however, was a priority. Indeed, with constrictive wartime shortages, completion of the Rochester spur was delayed—as deadlines approached, work along the Genesee River at the harbor and terminal facilities was shifted from the spur to the main line to ensure the Barge Canal would open on

The Court Street Dam was built in Rochester to control the Genesee River for navigation. The dam is in the center of this 1922 view; the Rochester Terminal is on the left bank of the canal behind the dam. Canal boats are tied along the canal wall and the railroad runs behind the terminal.

New York State Archives

time. Access to downtown Rochester was maintained in the meantime by keeping open a section of the Enlarged Erie Canal through the city and by connecting it to the Barge Canal at eastern and western points. A junction lock was needed at the western end since the water level of new canal was now at a higher elevation than the nineteenth-century Erie.

Because it was the last uncompleted portion, work on this section of the Barge became intense. "At the guard-lock east of the Genesee River . . . was enacted the most dramatic scene of all. Night and day, the men worked and on the morning of May 15, with the incoming canal water rising around their waists the final work was done."[8] Dramatically, Rochester became the last link in the new canal.

IRONDEQUOIT CREEK EMBANKMENT

The great embankment over the Irondequoit Creek was an engineering feat left over from the days of Clinton's Ditch a century earlier. Mounting the canal on a large earth path high across the Irondequoit Creek valley was an inspiring site in the early 1800s. When the time came to put through the Barge Canal, the same technique was used again, with only a slight route change. The earlier canal's embankment curved too sharply

The concrete trough of the Irondequoit Creek Embankment was nearing completion when this 1911 picture was taken.   *New York State Archives*

for the large barges of the new canal; the new embankment was raised south of its predecessor on a straighter course. The contractor used hydraulic dredges to pump material from a nearby ridge to the top of the embankment, then washed it down in place with industrial water hoses.

With hydraulic dredges and industrial waterhoses, earth was repositioned into the new embankment. Some material was used to form a bench on the south side of the embankment (which would become Jefferson Road). The bank, begun in May 1909, was completed two years later. In 1911 the canal's channel was begun on top, using poured concrete for the floors and walls. The walls were backfilled and by April 1912 the trough appeared ready for navigation. Following the huge break that washed out part of the embankment in September of that year, safeguards were added: The concrete floor was reinforced with layers of concrete and water that might seep from the bottom of the trough was directed through farm tile to the sidewalls.[9] By 1918 the embankment was restored and the crossing assumed its present appearance.

Siphon Lock in Oswego

Farther east at Oswego, the first *siphon lock* in this country (the third lock completed on the new system) was built at the northern terminus of the Oswego Barge Canal. Oswego Barge

By the time of this September 1912 photo, the trough of the Irondequoit Creek Embankment had been filled with water. Soon after, though, the culvert underneath it gave way and the trough collapsed.

Canal Society of New York State

Lock 8 used the force of air to empty and fill the lock instead of using gravity-driven water through electrically operated tunnels.

From the outside, the lock looked similar to other locks, except for the two large cement humps that formed the necks of the siphon on each lock wall. Under the hump, a vacuum formed in a pipe, which drew water into or out of the chamber. All the water going into or out of the lock went uphill over the crest of the siphons and the top of the lock walls. There was very little extra energy needed to operate the lock—most of the system was controlled by manipulating a four-inch air valve. Just 4.5 minutes were needed to fill the lock chamber; emptying it took just a bit longer.

The siphon technique required that air escape with each locking. Some of it escaped in small bubbles from the culvert ports in the lock, and some through air vents in the walls of the chamber, which could be a spectacular sight. Said one observer, "At first there is a discharge of mingled air and water, which is thrown a few feet from the lock wall, but as the flow through the siphon increases, the jets also increase until they occasionally blow a cloud of spray 50 or 60 feet."[10]

Siphon locks had been recommended for all of the shorter lift locks on the Barge Canal where a head of water was constant year round. They were expected to have lower operational costs since no electricity was required and less metal was needed, qualities that were apparently especially appreciated in this lake-connecting lock. Why no others were built is unclear.

Lock 8 was adapted in 1943 by adding a vacuum pump. The lock was changed over to the more common electrical-mechanical system about 1968.

THE CANAL CHALLENGES ROME

Canal construction near Rome faced a number of notable challenges. Deciding where the canal should go was one. If the canal was routed along the existing line through the heart of the city, construction would force the demolition of many downtown buildings and would require high overhead bridges that would disrupt traffic. A new southern route would require substantial alterations to busy rail lines. The routing decision was preceded by years of discussion among state, city, and railroad officials. Finally, the southern route was chosen, with the canal traveling straight west to reconnect with the old Erie at New London. In hindsight, the relocated New York Central line was probably an improvement: A new station was built, and both the canal and

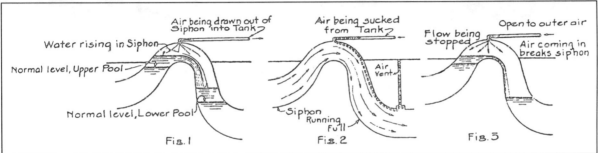

Air being drawn out of
Siphon into Tank

Water rising in Siphon

Normal level, Upper Pool

Normal level, Lower Pool

Fig. 1

Air being sucked
from Tank

Air Vent

Siphon
Running
Full

Fig. 2

Flow being
stopped

Open to outer air

Air coming in
breaks siphon

Fig. 5

the railroad were straightened, shortened, and taken out of the built-up section of Rome.

Historically, Rome has been the summit level of the Erie Canal, a distinction that presents its own problems. At either end of the summit, water flows down and away to lower elevations, therefore enough water has to be brought to the summit to fill not only the channel but also to compensate for this drain. The summit of the original Erie was 60 miles long, stretching from Frankfort to Syracuse. The Enlarged Erie reduced this to the distance between Utica and Syracuse. The Barge Canal lowered the summit 10 feet and shortened it to the 15 miles between Locks 20 and 21.

The state had to make provision for a large and constant flow of water for this section. The channel and locks of the Barge were obviously much larger than their predecessors, and required more water. The water supply includes many nineteenth-century sources, such as the reservoir system of the Black River Canal (to

Above:
Top: The siphon lock in Oswego was the only one of its kind on the Barge Canal. The gates operated by the movement of air through siphons. The identifying humps on the walls of Lock 8 in this 1922 view (looking northeast) are the only outward signs that the lock operated differently from others on the system.   *New York State Archives*
Bottom: By manipulating a four-inch air valve at Oswego Barge Lock 8, a siphon was created and water ran freely into the lock. By introducing air into the system, the siphon was broken and the lock stopped filling.

     Barge Canal Book of Plans (1920)

Due to the building of Delta Reservoir, the Black River Canal was moved alongside the reservoir instead of remaining in the flooded area. This 1921 view of the reservoir's dam shows the re-aligned Black River Canal in the foreground with its new aqueduct and locks, which were only used for a short time before the canal was abandoned for navigation.   *New York State Archives*

the north of Rome) and the southern system of Oneida, Chittenango, Limestone, and Jamesville Creeks (along with the Limestone and Jamesville reservoirs). Two new supplies were added: Delta Reservoir (at the headwaters of the Mohawk River) and Hinckley Reservoir (at the headwaters of West Canada Creek).

DELTA DAM AND RESERVOIR

Delta Dam created a reservoir that covered 4.3 square miles of the town of Western in Oneida County, including the village of Delta. The state removed its 295 buildings, and relocated nearby cemeteries and several miles of the Black River Canal. Four new locks and a new aqueduct were constructed for the latter, the remains of which can be seen today just below and along the east side of the dam.

The dam, five miles north of Rome, stands 100 feet higher than the rock at the base. It probably could have been higher, but "the height of the crest was fixed by a desire to avoid serious incursions upon the large and attractive village of Westernville at the head of the reservoir."[11] The dam is over 1,000 feet long, with a 300-foot-long spillway near its center. The concrete face of the dam extends 10 feet below the river bottom so that a permanent pool breaks the force of water passing over the dam.

The dam was placed at a narrow part of a rock-walled gorge just below a widening in the Mohawk River Valley. (The distinctive triangular shape of the valley floor gave the village its name, after the Greek letter delta.)[12] The reservoir recreates an ancient glacial lake that once occupied the landscape here; in fact, when the dam's foundation was excavated, a buried gorge, pot holes and other evidences of glacial erosion were found. The reservoir's average depth is about 23 feet.[13]

HINCKLEY DAM AND RESERVOIR

About 20 miles north of Utica is Hinckley Dam, which holds the water back in West Canada Creek. The dam is longer than the one at Delta because there was no advantageous narrow gorge to use as at the other location. The dam is about 82 feet high and 3,700 feet long, of which 400 feet is all concrete; the rest is an earthen embankment over a concrete core. The reservoir behind the dam covers nearly 4.5 square miles to an average depth of 28 feet.[14] The reservoir is named for the village just below the dam. (Three villages were covered by the impounded water; the state moved 209 buildings.)

Because the natural channel of West Canada Creek reaches the Mohawk River below the summit level of the canal, the water from the reservoir would be of no use to the summit. Therefore, a five-mile diversion channel was built to direct reservoir water to Nine Mile Creek, which empties into the Barge Canal on the summit level. The dam receives substantial runoff because of its advantageous location close to the Adirondack Mountains.

This reservoir, like Delta, also assists in flood control. The dams hold back high water in spring and then discharge it at a more reasonable rate. Unlike Delta, the Hinckley Dam provides hydroelectric power through the Gregory B. Jarvis Hydroelectric Plant, which began generating power in June 1986 under an agreement between the state's canal officials and the New York Power Authority. As part of the agreement, the Power Authority assumed maintenance responsibilities for the dam. The station is named for a Challenger space shuttle astronaut who grew up in nearby Mohawk.

THE HIGH LIFT LOCK AT LITTLE FALLS

The 40.5-foot lift at Erie Barge Lock 17 in Little Falls is the largest single lock on the Barge Canal. In fact, at the time of its construction it was the highest single lift lock in the world. This

The walls for the side pool at Lock 17 in Little Falls are being built in this 1912 view. Little Falls has the highest lift on the Barge Canal, and it was first thought the pool would be needed to be sure the lock filled as quickly as others. Notice the towpath for the Enlarged Erie Canal on the wooden planks around the lock. While the Barge was being built, boats were still operating on the old canal and the towpath was there to take boats past the construction site.

Canal Society of New York State

one lift accomplishes what five locks did at Little Falls on the Enlarged Erie Canal.

An interesting feature of this lock is that the lower gate is a *guillotine gate*. Instead of two side-by-side gates closing together into a mitered seam (as on most other Barge Canal locks), this single gate drops into place vertically (as the gate is lowered a counterweight is raised, one of the more dramatic scenes on the system). That huge steel gate hanging overhead probably has given many boaters pause. "I always thought the gate would come down and cut my boat in half," said Bill Hills of his time on a barge in the 1930s.[15] There are only two other locations with lock gates like this: the guard locks at the Genesee River crossing and the lock to the Utica harbor. At neither location are the gates as large, however.

Naturally, a lock this large requires an enormous volume of water to fill it. As part of its original design, Lock 17 included a novel solution to water conservation (which would have been critical if traffic on the system had reached the levels hoped for when the new canal was proposed): The lock was constructed with a storage pool on its south side to collect the top half of the water when the chamber was emptied for a locking. This water was then reused to help fill the chamber for a later locking. The pool eventually was removed when traffic needs never

A LONG HAUL

materialized. The large volume of water now empties from the 40.5-foot drop with such force that the water below the lower gates churns violently.

The falls for which Little Falls is named are on the other side of Moss Island from the lock at the focus of a dramatic narrowing of the Mohawk Valley. The approach to Little Falls from either direction brings the boater through a spectacular rocky gorge that has impressed travelers from the first days of the canal. These same rocky conditions, however, plagued the canal's builders. James D. Casey, one of the owners of the company that had the contract for Lock 17, was hit by falling rock in September 1909 during construction. He died a week later.[16]

In this view of Lock 17 in the mid-1930s the side pool has been emptied.Use of the pool was discontinued due to the low level of traffic on the canal. The pool's eastern wall, in the foreground, was later removed. The south wall of Lock 17 is to the right.
New York State Museum (Scothon Collection)

THE VISCHER FERRY AND CRESCENT DAMS

The dams at Vischer Ferry and Crescent, about 10 miles apart on the Mohawk River, are notable because of their size and because they are the only fixed dams on the main line of the Erie Barge. Unlike the movable dams elsewhere in the Mohawk Valley, these are permanent, year-round structures. Like the movable dams, though, they raise the water high enough for navigation, and in doing so they impound water that "spread out into virtual lakes."[17]

A TRULY AMAZING CONSTRUCTION

Right:
This overview of the Crescent Dam shows the two curved sections and rock island that make up its semi-circle. Below the dam is the Cohoes Falls (not shown). The upper right corner of the drawing shows where the Waterford flight of the Barge Canal meets the river. The old Enlarged Erie is marked in the left corner.

Barge Canal Book of Plans (1920)

Below:
The Vischer Ferry Dam is made up of three sections, two in the river and one across an island. The dam is in the Mohawk River east of Schenectady, and is 2,000 feet long. The middle section of the dam straddles a rock outcropping, seen clearly in this 1922 photo. Erie Lock 7 is on the far side of the river.

New York State Archives

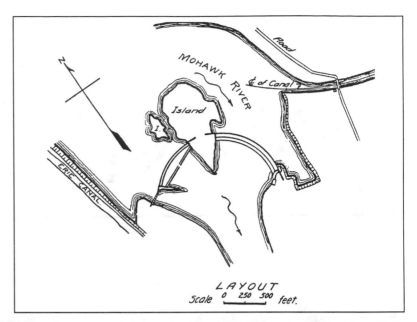

At the Vischer Ferry Dam (named for a nearby Saratoga County hamlet east of Schenectady), the river is divided into two channels by an island; the dam crosses the island and the channels in a "Z" shape. The top of the dam is 2,000 feet long at 36 feet above the apron, or base of the dam. Lock 7 is the southern end of the dam. There briefly was a lock at the northern end (where the Vischer Ferry hydroelectric station is now) that was used to allow navigation to continue on the old Enlarged Erie channel below and above the dam before the Waterford flight was completed.[18]

Just before the canal leaves the Mohawk River and enters the land line leading through the Waterford flight is Crescent Dam. It was built in two curved sections separated by a rocky prominence. The entire structure makes a semi-circle with a total length of just under 2,000 feet. The top of the dam is 39 feet above the apron; below the dam, a smaller dam forms a pool that protects the rocky base from being eroded by water coming over the dam.[19]

There is a large hydroelectric power station at the southern end of Crescent Dam. Like the one at Vischer Ferry, the station was built by the state soon after the completion of the Barge Canal, and both were operated by the state's canal department until the 1980s, when they were transferred to the New York Power Authority. The current Crescent facility replaced a much smaller powerhouse that once stood at the north end of the dam. This latter powerhouse (now gone) was part of the original design of the Barge Canal; it supplied, as the larger one still does, power for the two guard gates and the Waterford locks. The Waterford canal shops also receive power from the Crescent facility.[20]

THE WATERFORD FLIGHT

Through the years, whenever people have talked about traveling the Mohawk Valley west from the Hudson they have always been challenged with the first step of getting out of the Hudson Valley: how to get up and over the Cohoes Falls. Before the Erie Canal was built, commerce went overland to Schenectady and on to the Mohawk River in order to bypass this obstacle. The nineteenth-century canal worked its way around the falls in a

The Waterford flight consists of five locks within a mile and a half that lift boats a total of 169 feet. This c.1918 view is of locks 4, 5 and 6.

New York State Archives

This panoramic view of Lock 5 on the Waterford flight shows one of the pools built to compensate for the short distance between locks on the flight. This pool is needed to absorb the water released from Lock 6 so it doesn't overrun Lock 5. It also ensures that there is enough water to fill Lock 5. The piers in the pool guide boats between the locks.

New York State Archives

lock-laden stretch through the community of Cohoes, along the Mohawk's south shore. With good reason, this time-consuming portion of the Erie was the impetus for one of the nation's first railroads to develop a quicker overland route to Schenectady that would easily (and very successfully) compete with that last eastern leg of the Erie.

The route of the Erie Barge abandoned the nineteenth-century route in favor of a natural valley in a slightly more inland and northerly location. (Other options were considered, including a compact flight of locks immediately along the Mohawk's north bank.) The Waterford flight climbs up this landscape with lifts varying from 32.5 to 34.5 feet. Locks 2 through 6, having a combined lift of 169 feet, were known as the "greatest series of high lift locks in the world" when they were built.[21]

The locks are not connected, as are the tandem structures at Lockport and Seneca Falls, but are spaced out over a mile and a half, separated by large pools or ponds. Around each lock, a bypass channel lets water continue down the flight independent of the locks, assuring each pool has sufficient water. The pools serve to store water for lockages and to buffer the surges of water that occur when a lock is emptied. They calm a condition that often disrupted traffic on the nineteenth-century canal through Cohoes—the draw of water for the many tightly-spaced lockages on the older canal was at times great enough to completely use up the supply fed from above; conversely, the locks were so close that when a lock was emptied the water often flooded over the gate below.

The Waterford flight includes two guard gates at the western end to protect both the locks and the communities below from the catastrophe that would occur if one of the lock gates failed or an embankment washed out—all of the stored water in the Mohawk River would come flooding down to the Hudson through the village of Waterford. The second guard gate was installed after the state engineer had witnessed the volume and violence of the flood of 1913 and ordered the second gate installed.[22]

The locks at Waterford do not generate power. The defunct powerhouses at Locks 3 and 5 converted power from the generators at Crescent Dam from alternating to direct current.

The State's regional dry dock and maintenance shops are at Lock 3 in Waterford. The complex began with a boathouse (now gone), built in 1917 along the lock's western approach wall; a brick shop building was completed in 1922, the same year that shops were authorized in Pittsford and Baldwinsville (later moved to Syracuse). The dry dock was in use by 1925 and continues as the winter home for the state's maintenance fleet. During the season, the dry dock serves as a yard for the emergency repair of state-owned or private boats.

Before boats enter the Mohawk River from the Waterford flight, they pass through this impressive rock cut. The guard gate in the distance protects the village of Waterford and the flight from the Mohawk River if lock gates in the flight fail. This 1922 view shows a fleet of steel barges at the top of the flight, heading west. *New York State Archives*

5 Some Common Sights on the Canal

Although the placid waters of the Barge Canal are pleasant to look at, much effort goes into creating that apparent calm. Interrupting the canal water's horizon, the locks invite the most questions. "In point of interest, perhaps the locks take first place among canal structures," stated an observer at the time of their construction.[1]

Indeed, much canal architecture is interesting to look at but difficult to understand at first glance. The locks, movable dams, guard gates, and lift bridges are the main elements of the canal that are commonly watched and experienced. To appreciate how the canal operates today, these are the key structures to study.

LOCKING THROUGH

All of the locks on the Barge Canal operate similarly. The ones on the river sections are next to dams; the locks allow vessels to get past the dams. On the land-cut sections, the locks lift or lower vessels past natural changes in terrain and elevation. Most locks have two pairs of gates, tunnels within the side walls for water to pass through, and a rectangular chamber about 328 feet long and 45 feet wide.

Erie Barge Lock 23 near Brewerton is the busiest lock on the system. Located just west of Oneida Lake, it sees so much traffic because recreational boaters and anglers from the Syracuse metropolitan area regularly use Oneida Lake and Sylvan Beach on the eastern shore. The chief lock operator at Lock 23, Bill Pittsley, says that "anyone who lives around here and has a boat has been through the lock."[2] This lock is a good example to study to better understand the workings of all 58 locks on the canal system.

If a boat leaves Oneida Lake and goes west toward Syracuse or Oswego on the canal, the boat enters the Oneida River from the lake and then goes into a land-cut section of canal before getting to Lock 23. The boat enters the full lock with the far western gates closed, the water in the lock at the same level as the water in the

Opposite:
As the movable dam at Cranesville was built, the frames for the dam panels were put in place. These frames, shown here in 1910, are pulled completely out of the water during the winter to let the river take its natural path.

New York State Archives

river and lake behind. (From Oneida Lake west to the Lake Ontario plain the terrain goes downhill, thus Lock 23 lowers boats heading west.) Once the boat enters the 45-foot-wide, steel-lined concrete lock chamber, the crew ties a rope from the boat to one of 12 snubbing posts along the side of the lock to keep the boat from moving around uncontrollably in the currents caused by the water draining from the lock chamber. A warning bell rings and the eastern gates behind begin their deliberate, steady close. These upper (upstream) gates weigh about 50 tons; they're shorter than the 100-ton lower (downstream) gates. Both gates consist of steel doors that come together in a vertical watertight seal. When the gates close, they make a heavy "thunk" like the secure sound of a closing safe. The lock operator closes the gates by moving brass control handles in a small white booth at the side of the lock.

After the operator closes the lock gates, the valves at each end of the lock that control the flow of water in the tunnels in the walls of the lock are gradually opened; after the upper gates are closed, the lock operator walks down to the lower, western end of the lock and opens the valves at that end to allow water to flow out of the lock, into the tunnel, and out to the western level of the canal. When the water in the lock has drained so that it's at

In 1921, it was common to see steam tugs and wooden barges such as the *Crescent*, built in 1894, with her fleet at Erie Lock 23.   *New York State Archives*

A LONG HAUL

the same level as the water on the other side of the lower gate — about seven feet lower than on the Oneida Lake side — the lower gates are opened. (As the water level on each side of the lower gates equalizes, the gates shift a little, a visual signal that lets the operator know when to open the gates.)

For a boat traveling east (upstream), the process is reversed: The operator closes the lower valves and opens the upper ones to let water into the lock from the upstream side until it is the same as the upper level. This entire process is called a *locking*. At Lock 23, sometimes 10 pleasure boats at a time may be contained in one locking.

A small crowd often gathers on the edge of the lock to watch the locking process, a scene that has been repeated many times over the years at the locks on the canal. A 1961 description of Erie Lock 17 at Little Falls is a good example: "An exceptionally large number of out-of-town and out-of-state visitors were seen standing along the walls of the lock and spillways watching a number of pleasure boats and barges as they were lifted and lowered a distance of 40.5 feet between the water levels. Cameras clicked away as the lifting and lowering took place."[3] Crowds still gather at the locks today, as do the boats. "There is always traffic waiting

These days, pleasure boats are a common sight in Lock 23.

Author's collection.

Who Uses This Lock?

In 1995, Lock 23 averaged 50 lockages a day in the summer. (A *lockage* is whenever the lock has to be emptied to transfer a boat to the next level; the term does not necessarily reflect the number of boats using the lock.) Because most of the boats today are relatively small pleasure craft, quite a few can fit in one lockage. There were 8,924 boats locked through in 1995—almost twice as many as the next busiest lock, Lock 7 near Schenectady on the Erie Barge Canal, which had 4,724 boats go through. Most locks did not see more than 2,000 boats during the year. Lock 28A in Wayne County had less than 1,000.[5]

Almost all the 1995 traffic was pleasure boats. The most notable exceptions were the tug *Honey*, which came through about twice a month pushing calcium carbonate, and the *Mayan Prince* and *Emita II*, both commercial cruise boats. In 1995 there were just over 100 commercial lockings, including tour boats; a decade earlier, the number was eight time greater. In a one-week period in September 1965, a host of commercial vessels went through, including the *Day Peckinpaugh* (hauling cement); the tugs *Jessica Kehoe*, *Martha Moran*, *Morania*, and the *Evening Star*; and oil company craft like the *Mobil Albany* and *Mobil New York*. These boats even then shared the waterway with pleasure boats and, in fact, were outnumbered by them in 1965.[6]

The use today of Lock 23 by thousands of pleasure boats is reflected in another change in the day-to-day operation of the lock. The resumption of tolls for use of the canal led to the hiring of two collectors at the lock just to sell daily and seasonal passes in 1995. On some days, as many as 50 passes were sold at this lock.[7]

to go through when I get here in the morning," Pittsley says. "It's a very busy lock."[4]

Though activity at Lock 23 makes it an interesting one to watch, not as many people visit it as they do to locks located within cities or villages. Nonetheless, with a blanket of trees surrounding it and a park that draws picnickers all summer, the lock is very picturesque.

As boats pass through a lock, the operator waves and often stops to answer questions from people along the side. Lock operators today have become public-relations representatives, introducing the canal to visitors on both the land and water sides of the lock wall, a tradition that extends from the days of the commercial traffic in past decades. Commercial boaters moving east might inquire at Lock 23 to learn how conditions were on the sometimes-treacherous Oneida Lake because the operator would hear if a western-bound boat had trouble making the lake crossing (or he would check with the now-gone weather tower at Brewerton).

Lock 23 has a hydroelectric powerhouse with much of its early twentieth-century equipment intact. Standing on the northwest

corner of the lock, it is possibly the best preserved of the few
surviving canal hydroelectric stations. In the first days of the
Barge, the powerhouses provided all the electricity for the locks.
Many were torn down or their equipment removed in the 1950s
and 1960s, when alternative sources of power appeared cheaper
and when parts needed to maintain the equipment became
difficult to find. All locks on the Barge now depend on commercial sources for their primary power, though the old units
serve as emergency backups. Besides Lock 23, some other good
surviving powerhouses are at Lock 5 on the Champlain Barge
Canal, Lock 4 on the Cayuga and Seneca Barge Canal, and
Lock 28B on the Erie Barge. At these locations, water flowing
underneath the powerhouses operates turbines which turn two
electric generators, producing direct current. Lock 23 now only
generates power in the winter in order to run the historic
electric heaters in the powerhouse while the crew does
maintenance work.

At locks where there is not a sufficient year-round head of
water, a gasoline generator is used to provide backup power. The

The now-gone vertical generators in this
c.1918 view were located at Lock 6 on
the Champlain Barge Canal. Water that
went past the lock operated turbines
below the floor

Canal Society of New York State

Following pages:
The cross sections of two powerhouses,
one with a cone-shaped vertical
generator *(page 106)* and the other with
a horizontal generator *(page 107)*, show
how the water comes through the
tunnel in the lock wall to turn a
turbine. An example of a vertical
generator is at Champlain Canal Lock
5; a horizontal generator is still used at
Erie Lock 23.

Barge Canal Book of Plans (1920)

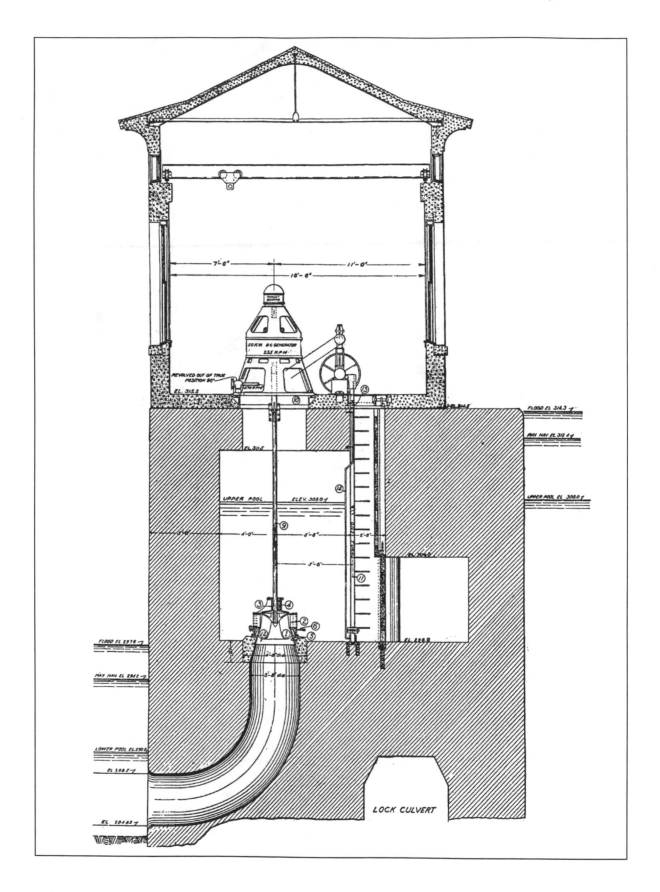

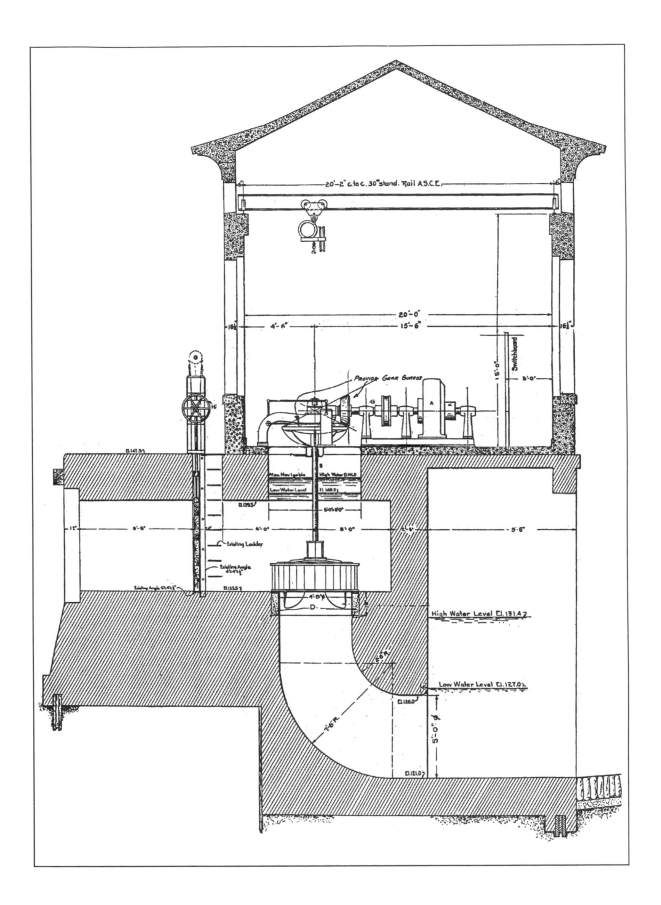

Mohawk River locks are the most common examples of this because there is no hydroelectric generating potential when the dams are raised at the end of each season. These locks received gasoline generators when first built, some of which have since been replaced with more modern, gasoline-driven generators.

Lock 23 has been honored a number of times as a prize lock on the Barge Canal System, part of an annual competition that began in 1915. Locks on the system are inspected twice a year, and first-, second-, and third-place awards are given. In 1941 Lock 23 won third prize; in 1933, 1935, 1946, and 1962 it won second place; in 1976, 1980, and 1984 it captured first prize. Each award is a credit to the lock operators, who are responsible for making the locks both look and run well. Some operators seem to have a natural gift for keeping the lock up, said 39-year veteran of the canal Dennis Fishette, an electrical supervisor and the official responsible for inspecting the locks from 1990 through 1995.

Lock operators must have pride in their work. In a few cases they learned how to operate the lock from a father or uncle, a family tradition that reinforces a sense of pride in the appearance and operation of the lock. Fishette, whose grandparents were Italian immigrants who helped dig the Barge Canal, started on the canal in 1956 as a general laborer, eventually working on his father's lock—Lock 33. "Since 1929, there hasn't been a day my father or I haven't been on the canal," Fishette said a year before his 1994 retirement.

Another second-generation lock operator was the late Cal Pendergrass, who climbed up the state's ranks to work on Lock 17 in Little Falls, the lock next to the one his father had worked. Pendergrass said in a 1976 interview that when the Barge Canal opened, his father "took the examination for lock operator . . . passed . . . and he got the job at Lock 18 at Jacksonburg, and he could walk to work." The younger Pendergrass worked for a time at the Jacksonburg lock before moving to Lock 17. He noted that in 1961, 12 to 16 barges a day passed through the lock.[8]

Then there's the late Clarence Taylor, former chief at Lock 33 in Brighton. He was a local who hung around Lock 33 when it was being built and was hired on as a night watch. When the lock was completed, he became the operator with minimal extra training, Dennis Fishette recalled. Taylor had such an intense pride and feeling of ownership of his lock that when Fishette started working for him there, Taylor told Fishette that "you'll never last more than three weeks" because of the high standards that he set. He was a demanding chief lock operator: Before leaving his lock to the night shift he put matchsticks in key

places to be sure that every part of the lock was inspected by his relief person; the sticks fell away after the inspections had been done as they should.[9]

More typical lock operators, though, are people like Bill Pittsley, who was exposed to the canal through a seasonal work program and took a liking to it. Pittsley worked at a number of locks since 1987, including Lock 29 in Palmyra and Lock 5 on the Oswego Canal at Minetto. He has been at Lock 23 since October 1995.

In the peak years of the canal—the 1950s—lock operators rarely had a moment's rest. "It was so busy, I remember having barges sitting at each end of the lock, waiting their turn to go through," Fishette said.[10] The operators often became familiar, even welcomed parts of their canal environment for the boat crews that made regular and frequent trips through the system. At Erie Barge Lock 19 there was a store in the lock house geared for the commercial boaters; at Lock 21, there was a grocery stand that tugboat captain Fred Godfrey recalled. (He heard the store was closed when the assistant lock operators complained about doing the work to keep up the store but getting none of the profits.) Canal officials did not endorse these entrepreneurial operations. Often, there would be informal exchanges of food between the boats and the lock operators: The lock operators would offer samplings of fresh produce such as tomatoes, corn, and baked goods, and, in return, the commercials would pass them dinner

Valves control the water that flows through the tunnels in the walls of the lock. These men are re-installing a valve in Lock 17 in the mid 1930s. The valves are vertical and the flanged wheels help the valve move on tracks that run inside the lock wall.

New York State Museum (Scothon Collection)

cooked in the galleys of the boats or offer to meet them for a beer if the barge was tied up for the night. Both the lock operators and the barge crews had nicknames for each other as they passed. "Hey, horse thief!" a barge deckhand might call out to the lock operator. "Hey, nightmare!" the operator would retort.[11]

A post office of sorts was set up at several locks. "The mailing service at Lock 17, which has been in operation since 1911, is one

A *lock operator's typical day*

Daily Lockage Report   Erie Canal Lock 19   November 28, 1932

Time Lockage Completed	Number of boats	Tug or Boat Name
12:15 AM	2	*St. Lowery*, 1 barge
1:00	2	*K. Moran* and *Tex.* 158
1:30	1	*Amsterdam SOCONY*
2:35	3	*Cornell* and 2 barges
3:20	4	4 barges
3:50	1	*Mabel*
4:15	1	*I.L.I.* 101
6:15	1	*Buffalo SOCONY*
8:00	1	*Maple Leaf*
9:10	1	*L.T.C. #2*
10:15	1	*Metropolitan*
11:00	3	*Linda T., D. Boat #1*
12:30 PM	3	*Buffalo* and 2 barges
1:10	4	2 barges, *T.2.,B.B.*120
1:35	2	*T.2* and scow
2:15	3	*S. Cross* and 2 barges
2:50	2	2 barges
3:35	3	*Pine Grove*, 2 barges
4:20	2	2 barges
5:30	4	*Cornell #20*, 3 barges
6:00	3	3 barges
6:35	2	*Dauntless #5*, 1 barge
8:10	3	*V. Kelley*, 2 barges
8:45	2	2 barges
9:35	1	Tug *Coyne*
10:05	1	*Rome SOCONY*
12:00 AM	1	*Hartford SOCONY*

of four strategic points along water routes," a 1961 observer stated. Mailboxes were located at Oswego, Waterford, and Whitehall to serve the many geographic areas of the canal system.[12] At the federal lock in Troy, informal post office boxes were in the lock house until World War II prohibited access to the lock beyond the chamber walls.

Visitors to Lock 17 in 1961 "watched boatmen as they leaped from their boats and dashed to the row of 25 mailboxes, located on the side of the building, and covered with a canopy to protect them." The variously sized mailboxes sat on two wooden shelves and were put there by the "different companies operating tugboats and barges on the waterways."[13] Even the official Little

The empty chamber of Lock 6 on the Champlain Canal during rehabilitation in 1998 shows the holes visible along the bottom of the lock walls. Water comes into and out of the chamber through these holes when the lock is filling and emptying.

New York State Museum

Falls Post Office put a mailbox there so the crews could mail letters. Since the boat crews had no home base for weeks at a time, these mailboxes were a vital service so crews could keep in touch with their families and receive important papers (like their paychecks).

Additionally, lock operators and their seasonal helpers keep the locks looking like parks, with flowers, fresh paint, and mowed grass, a long tradition at the locks. A 1933 log book from Lock 5 on the Champlain Barge Canal includes an April 18 entry that the lock operator was "spading and planting flower beds [and] raking [the] lawn." The day before, the operator had set out bulbs. Today, the federal government's Greenthumb program sponsors summer help from nearby communities to help with these activities.

The life preserver found at every lock is not there just for decoration. Dennis Fishette remembered in 1968, when he was the chief at Lock 33, a young child was riding a tricycle near the lock. His mother began calling, "Timmy, Timmy come here. Where are you?" The boy answered, "In the lock." By the time Fishette got to the edge of the lock with the life preserver he could only see a patch of hair in the water. He jumped in. The lock was at the low level, but that still meant 15 feet of water. Fishette managed to save the boy and receive a commendation for his efforts.[14]

In another incident that same year at Erie Barge Lock 18 (between Herkimer and Little Falls), a lock worker had a fainting spell and fell into the lock's valve pit, one of four 3-foot by 6-foot holes in the lock wall that lead down to the water discharge tunnels. The man fell 18 feet into the pit, which was filled with 15 feet of water. Another lock worker scrambled down the chains in the pit to the ladder and then into the water to save his coworker. Both survived, and the men who helped in the rescue also received a commendation.[15]

Locks are staffed all winter, even though the canal itself is closed to navigation. There are many jobs to do which cannot be done when the canal is operating, from cleaning machinery to painting to general maintenance.[16] Many parts of the lock are disassembled and cleaned, painted, and lubricated. A sampling from the 1956 log book at Champlain Barge Lock 5 outlines some of the jobs done on the lock in the winter: cleaning the brass, painting screen doors and window casings, adjusting bearings, shoveling snow, fixing the head gate, dismantling and cleaning the pump motor, checking the generator, installing an electric line for the pump, working on the water wheel,

Opposite:
Top: Guards were stationed at locks during World War I to protect the structures from sabotage. This guard is at Erie Lock 3 in Waterford.
New York State Archives
Bottom: It was not just the locks that were guarded during World War I. This guard is in front of the West Shore Railroad bridge over the canal in Pittsford in 1917.   *New York State Archives*

SOME COMMON SIGHTS ON THE CANAL

113

removing ice from the pit, painting ladders, and painting and cleaning the power house.

The canal was completed in the midst of World War I, and this brought more challenges to its operation. Military guards were placed at strategic points on the canal, where "by using explosives, the waterway could be so damaged as to cause long interruptions in navigation as well as large financial loss."[17] Details of soldiers camped along the locks, and canal officials tried to make them comfortable during their long stays in sometimes remote places. At some locks, guard houses were erected. (At Erie Barge Lock 17, the former chief operator, Cal Pendergrass, recalled that the lock's garage and another building at the lock "were built during World War I for guards . . . All your locks had guards on them, soldiers of course . . . After the soldiers moved out after the war, the state took the buildings over.")[18] Visitors were not allowed to visit the locks.

In World War II, the country was again concerned that the enemy would try to sabotage the nation's transportation systems. The log book of Champlain Barge Lock 5 includes a number of references to blackouts at the lock in 1943. A 1940 newspaper article states that in recognition of the war's threat to a

By the spring of 1910, bridge work of the movable dam at Cranesville was being erected. Train travelers along the Mohawk River mistook these structures for bridges with extra support.

New York State Archives

A LONG HAUL

This c.1918 picture of a typical movable "mule" with winch was taken at Lock 15 in Fort Plain. The winch moves along the length of the movable dam, raising or lowering the gates as needed.

Canal Society of New York State

still-neutral United States, the "Barge Canal locks will be termed guarded areas and 'helpers' will be placed on night duty at each lock. 'No trespass' signs will be posted soon."[19] Other canal structures were of concern as well: A March 16, 1941, article says that "cameras and camera shots are now prohibited near the Barge Canal, Delta Dam or other public utility properties."[20]

MOVABLE DAMS: IT'S TIME TO PULL THE UPPERS

Another familiar site along the canal, especially on the Mohawk River, are the movable dams. They often look like bridges, though without the expected roadways along the banks. An unusual site even now, they were even more startling when they were first constructed. A contemporary description notes that "most conspicuous of the canal structures are the great steel trusses, which the bridge builders have thrown across the river this summer. But probably not more than one out every hundred that see them realizes that they are other than ordinary bridges, and so it is scarcely strange that the steel frames now being hung below the bridge floors should seem puzzling. Indeed, one traveler was recently overheard explaining that the superstructure was found so weak that it required the addition of these props to strengthen it."[21]

Some of the movable dams have two spans; a few have three. The spans vary in length from 150 to 240 feet, with the total length of the dams ranging from 370 to 590 feet. The movable dam at Rotterdam Junction, with its adjoining Lock 9, consists of three spans—two are 150 feet long, one is 210 feet long. Boats coming from the east are raised 15 feet into the level of the pool formed by the dam.

The feature that makes the Rotterdam Junction dam exceptional is that there is a roadway across the dam (the only other such roadway is at Lock 13 at Tribes Hill). There also is an unused walkway on the dam at Lock 10 at Cranesville that was installed to allow workers from Amsterdam to reach their jobs at the Adirondack Power and Light plant on the south shore. Noble Whitford noted that "although the bridges were built primarily to function only as parts of the dams, they were inherently capable of serving as highway bridges . . . Some of them are situated where highway bridges across the river would be most acceptable to the inhabitants."[22]

As is typical of the Mohawk movable dams, no water is left at the Rotterdam Junction site come winter; the metalwork of the dams is lifted completely out and the Mohawk River is allowed to resume its natural course. The canal planners had to consider the intense development on the banks of the river—the result of the many years that the Mohawk Valley has served as a great natural highway between the Hudson River and the Great Lakes. Fixed dams in the river would mean that "any change which might raise the height of floods in a territory thus highly developed would both cause serious injury and annoyance, and would also result in attendant suits for damage."[23]

On the river bed at the base of each of the dams are concrete sills (which stay year-round) stretching the width of the river. In the spring, steel frames (which have been drawn underneath the bridge for the winter) are swung down, using chains, and lowered into the concrete sills. The frames are 15 feet apart and each contains an upper and a lower steel gate, or plate; the plates in the frames form the basis of the dam. The bottoms of the lower gates rest on the sill while the tops of the upper gates form the crest of the dam. The gates work like a window sash: They roll on a track on the frame and can be raised or lowered to adjust the amount of water going past the dam. For instance, during heavy rain and high water, the lock operator will pull some of the upper gates to allow more of the water through the larger gap formed between the upper and lower gates. The operator can pull as many gates as necessary to achieve the correct water level.

Before doing this, though, the operator must first notify the locks down river: If the operator on an upstream lock opens the gates the resulting rush of water could quickly fill the river above the next lock. Some of the next downstream lock's gates have to be correspondingly raised, and so on downstream. This would be a reasonable procedure if it was done during the day in nice weather. Often, that is not the case. At times, high water occurs in the middle of the night and during a storm. Operators have to go out on the bridge and engage the winch on a trolley-like machine mounted on tracks known as the mule so that it can go the length of the dam to pull any of the gates.

Lock operators at the dams need to have the technical know-how to operate the machinery, but they also need to be able to "read" the river, a skill not easily learned from a training manual. Operators have to be able to judge if they should ride out the high water or whether they should indeed pull the uppers. The operator has to know if just a brief shower is causing the water to rise in the pool or if the rain will continue and raise the water for a long time, whether the pool can hold more water or if it is already close to its limits. These decisions were even more

High water or ice jams, such as this one in the Mohawk River in February 1922, would damage lock machinery if it was at ground level. The lock machinery is on the second floor of the concrete structures on either side of the lock. At these Mohawk River locks, the powerhouses, such as this one at Lock 8, are similarly located on high ground nearby.

New York State Museum (Scothon Collection)

difficult in past decades when timely and accurate weather forecasts were unavailable.

The operator also has to know exactly which gates to pull when the water is high, a decision that can affect the current below the lock. As a tug captain, Fred Godfrey remembers having to compensate for the power of the ever-present eddy when he entered the river locks—the eddy was always stronger as more gates were pulled. He saw a tug captain unfamiliar with the Mohawk dams and locks try to buck the current at Lock 14 at Canajoharie only to end up badly denting the oil barge he was pushing when it was pulled to the side as it entered the lock.

The electrical machinery that operates the locks by the dams is not contained in ground-level metal boxes alongside the lock, as at Lock 23; the machinery is on the upper level of the two-story cement structures rising from the sides of the lock—a safety measure to protect the machinery from winter or spring floods. (For the same reason, some of the powerhouses at these locks were located on high ground a short distance from the lock, such as the powerhouse that overlooks Erie Barge Lock 12.)

Some of the lock houses at the movable dams have photographs of their locks during high water. It is hard to believe that

This 1921 view of a guard gate at the top of Lock 3 on the Cayuga and Seneca Canal in Seneca Falls hangs like a guillotine over the water. This gate can be lowered to control water, especially if a break occurs. A brick powerhouse operated by New York State Electric and Gas next to the dam is on the left side of the scene.   *New York State Archives*

A LONG HAUL

relatively low water of summer can become such an angry force in the valley. But photos of huge blocks of ice on the top of the canal locks are undeniable evidence.

GUARD GATES: PROTECTION FROM ACCIDENTS

Guard gates are a type of movable dam, though they are seldom used when the canal is in use. They quickly isolate sections of the waterway in case of an emergency such as a break or extreme high water. Just over two dozen guard gates dot the Barge Canal system, nearly always sited to separate land-cut sections from river or lake portions of the canal. They are also regularly interspersed on the longer land-cut sections.

The guard gates consist of two towers on each side of the canal, with one or two steel gates suspended between. The gates are lowered with machinery usually situated on the steel bridge that goes across the gates, though sometimes the controls and machinery are located at the base of the gate. The machinery allows the gate to drop by manipulating two counterweight/pulley systems in the towers. There is a sill at the bottom of the canal beneath the gate on which the gate fits when it is lowered.

This guard lock is east of the Genesee River crossing in Rochester. If the river was too high or low, the guard lock gates would remain closed. Boats would have to go into the lock to overcome the change in water level. This 1921 view of the lock shows the cleared banks shortly after the canal opened.
New York State Archives

The guard gates are raised at the beginning of the season to let water into the land-cut sections; they are lowered at the end of the season so the canal can be drained for maintenance and for protection from spring floods. The gates are placed wherever a break could release a dangerously large volume of water from the canal if the section with the break was not isolated. For example, there is a guard gate in Pendleton near the western edge of the Erie Barge Canal. This gate is raised in the spring to allow Lake Erie water to fill the canal in the western part of the state; in the fall, the gate is dropped so that section of the canal can be drained.

There are two guard gates at the top of the Waterford flight to be doubly sure the Mohawk River could not suddenly drain down through Waterford and damage the five locks in the flight if there was a break. (Because of that fear, the Waterford gates are kept down even during the navigation season—an operator is stationed at the guard gates to open them for every approaching vessel.)

An excellent example of the emergency use of the guard gates occurred in 1972, when workers were digging under the great Irondequoit embankment at Bushnell's Basin. They weakened the underside of the embankment and it collapsed, causing torrents of water to flood out of the canal. One of the first things that was done was to drop the guard gates east and west of the site so only the water in the section between the gates would escape.

Two *guard locks* on the Barge Canal system could be considered a variation of the guard-gate theme. Now seldom used, these guard locks are at the Genesee River crossing. They include a traditional lock chamber with a guard gate at each end (instead of the more common, mitered V-shaped gates on lift locks, which only work when there is water pushing them closed from the upstream side). At a guard lock, high water could be on either side. At the Genesee crossing, the guard locks protect the canal from a river level that could be too high or low (conditions that could flood or drain an otherwise unprotected canal). Since the construction of the Mount Morris Dam south of the crossing, the river levels at this point have been stable and the locks are rarely needed.

LOW BRIDGE: RAISE 'ER UP!

A characteristic canal scene, especially in the western part of the Erie Barge Canal, includes a lift bridge spanning the canal, which is not surprising since there are more than a dozen lift bridges on the system. When the bridges are lowered to the road level (the position they're in most of the time), a stairway on each side of the bridge seems to go up about 10 feet to nowhere. Once the bridge is raised, however, the stairways connect to the level of the raised bridge. Below ground at one end of the bridge is a pit that holds the hydraulic or electric machinery used to raise the bridge on vertical racks and pinions. Another distinctive element of the lift bridges are the operator's houses on one of the adjoining banks. Many have been remodeled or replaced since their original early twentieth-century construction. Some are square; others are hexagonal.

In the earlier, busier days of the canal, an operator was stationed at each lift bridge 24 hours a day due to the nearly constant passing of tugs and barges. Today, though an occasional commercial vessel might get the bridge raised at night, the bridge's operation is normally kept within daytime hours. The Canal Corporation uses roving operators for the bridges—people in charge of more than one bridge who drive to each one when necessary. Boats traditionally give three blasts of their horns to alert the operator to raise the bridge; the operators also communicate with nearby locks and bridges so they know when a boat will soon be approaching the bridge. When it is time to lift the bridge, the operator rings a bell to alert the traffic on the road that the bridge is going up, and a gate goes down to block traffic on the road and sidewalk. (Cars and pedestrians are not allowed on the bridge while it is being lifted.)

In the western section of the Erie Barge Canal, lift bridges are a common sight. This 1921 view of the bridge at Lockport shows an operator's house.

New York State Archives

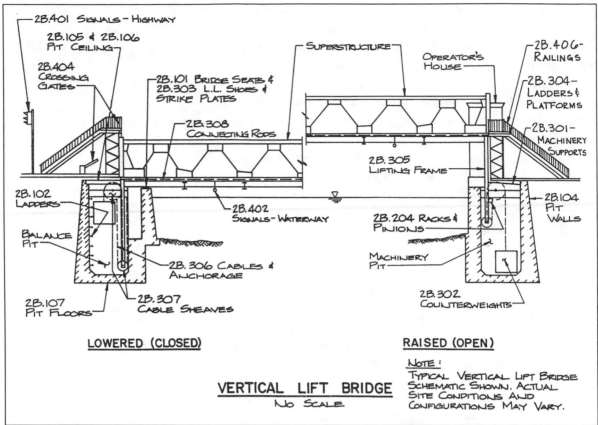

2B.401 SIGNALS - HIGHWAY

2B.105 & 2B.106 PIT CEILING

2B.404 CROSSING GATES

2B.101 BRIDGE SEATS & 2B.303 L.L. SHOES & STRIKE PLATES

SUPERSTRUCTURE

OPERATOR'S HOUSE

2B.406 - RAILINGS

2B.304 - LADDERS & PLATFORMS

2B.301 - MACHINERY SUPPORTS

2B.308 CONNECTING RODS

2B.305 LIFTING FRAME

2B.102 LADDERS

2B.402 SIGNALS - WATERWAY

2B.204 RACKS & PINIONS

2B.104 PIT WALLS

BALANCE PIT

2B.306 CABLES & ANCHORAGE

MACHINERY PIT

2B.107 PIT FLOORS

2B.307 CABLE SHEAVES

2B.302 COUNTERWEIGHTS

LOWERED (CLOSED)

RAISED (OPEN)

NOTE:
TYPICAL VERTICAL LIFT BRIDGE SCHEMATIC SHOWN. ACTUAL SITE CONDITIONS AND CONFIGURATIONS MAY VARY.

VERTICAL LIFT BRIDGE
NO SCALE

Above:

A lift bridge has a pit at each end—one for the operating machinery and the other as a balance pit. The right side of the diagram shows the bridge as if it is raised; the left side shows the bridge in the lowered position.

Canal Structure Inspection Manual (1993)

Right:

This 1921 view of the lift bridge in Spencerport shows the bridge at street level and the stairs by the operator's house left hanging at the level of the raised bridge. At the top of the stairs is a bell that rang when the bridge was raised. *New York State Archives*

The lift bridge in Fairport is an interesting example: It does not merely connect two sides of one roadway, but is built at an angle so it blocks traffic on two streets when it is raised. In 1957 the Fairport Chamber of Commerce proposed eliminating this nuisance in the middle of town, but the project smoldered for years because many in the town wanted to preserve the bridge. The 1914 structure remains in the village. It clears the water by just 6 feet when it is in the lowered position and by 15.75 feet in a raised position. It weights 685,909 pounds and spans 138.9 feet.[24]

There is an amusing story about the bridge that has circulated through the years. One foggy night, two village jokesters blew a boat whistle three times as they approached the lift bridge. The operator hurried to raise the bridge only to discover that the boaters were in a canoe which easily could have passed underneath the bridge. In another incident, the crew of a large boat thought they could pass underneath the bridge without raising the structure. Unfortunately, the boat was too big and it jammed under the bridge so tightly that the boat was stuck. It took a while to free the boat, and the repairs for both boat and bridge were expensive.

By 1978, as many as three boats an hour were passing under the bridge, making it one of the more active canal lift bridges. The increased use resulted from the recent development of nearby Fairport Village Landing.[25]

6   *The Floating Plant*

Just as the locks and movable dams are symbols of the Barge Canal's distinctive and enduring character, so the state's vintage yellow-trimmed blue boats are part of that heritage. As with so many other elements of canal life, the boats are not youngsters on the waterway. Many date to the first years of the Barge Canal; at least one predates it. With their steel hulls protected by rope fenders, the state's tugs also remind visitors of the canal when it was a waterway for commercial barges and tugs.

Once referred to as the "Empire State's Navy"[1], the state's floating plant includes the buoy boats, tugs and tug tenders, dredges, derrick boats, quarter boats, scows, and the self-propelled scows, all vividly displaying the state's blue-and-yellow colors. In 1995, there were more than 60 of the craft still in use throughout the length of the system.[2] These floating workhorses pull fallen trees and other debris out of the canal, dredge, move cumbersome equipment to a lock, and carry dignitaries on inspection tours, among other things. They also carry on a tradition of such noteworthy services as saving barges from capsizing on Oneida Lake or breaking ice so that tankers stuck in the canal could get to Syracuse for the winter. Canal workers who refer to these craft by name seem to do so as if they were part of the family, and when the vessels need repairs, the work is done meticulously.

The smallest state boats are the *buoy boats*, built to service the channel-marking buoys when kerosene lights were used. In 1926 there were 2,600 lighted navigational aids such as buoys, lighthouses, or beacons on the river and lake sections of the canal.[3] Each buoy was lit by one lamp that could hold three quarts of kerosene lasting about 31 hours.

Dan Geist, a retired tugboat captain from state service, was once a buoy tender. He and his buoy boat were responsible for 15 miles of canal with 90 to 100 lights. Along with checking the lights for fuel, he had to make sure the buoys remained upright. He remembered, "One person used a buoy as a water ski launch

Opposite:
The tugboat *Urger* was one of the workhorses of the state's fleet, here tied up at Waterford in 1941.

New York State Archives

The state tug *Schenectady* was the first tug to go through the Waterford locks on the opening day of the flight in 1915. It was originally the *George W. Aldridge*, built in 1896 for use by the state on the old canal. *Canal Society of New York State (Gayer Collection)*

by putting it on its side. Kids would try to turn the buoys over. Some kids kept turning over a buoy on Cross Lake." He painted the buoy with a mixture of paint and kerosene so it would stay sticky and discourage the kids from touching it. When he returned to the buoy, he was dismayed to see that the kids had written obscenities on it.[4]

The main job of the person operating the buoy boat was to travel a section of the canal to fill the lamps with kerosene and trim the wicks, but the tender also checked for debris in the water. Dennis Fishette remembered a summer he was on buoy duty. "Two lamps were placed on the deck of the boat. You would pull one out of the water and put a lit one back. We did the lamps on Monday, Tuesday, Thursday, and Friday. On Wednesday we stayed in to paint and repair the boat. It beat shoveling," he said, referring to a previous canal job he had—shoveling coal into the fire box of a tug. Recalling his love for the water, he said, "I couldn't believe they were paying me to do this."

He also said that most buoy tenders had another job because the pay was quite low—about equal to that of a laborer. Sometimes the buoy tenders were local farmers who could fit the buoy responsibilities in amid farm work. Dan Geist held two or three jobs at a time when he was a buoy tender. The number of jobs, though, "could get you into trouble if you couldn't keep up the buoy lights." Fishette said the job was a lonely one, "but most people liked it that way."[5]

A LONG HAUL

The buoy boats were originally made of wood, but they gradually were replaced by steel-hulled ones built in the late 1920s and 1930s at the state's Syracuse canal shops. Buoy boats that went on the lakes to maintain those buoys were longer and had slightly higher bows than the ones that worked the land-line sections. The buoy boats weighed four tons and were operated by hand-cranked gas engines (eventually converted to diesel engines). After 1970, buoys no longer used kerosene so no one needed to make the regular rounds with the boats anymore; the boats, looking like big rowboats with glassed huts on the deck, today are used for odd jobs on the canal.

Now the buoys are not lit at all—they're simply smaller reflective posts that float, though they still have to be set in the spring and pulled in the fall. To set the buoys in the spring, crews are first sent out to find markings on the banks of the canal that indicate where the buoys should be placed. They also use navigational maps that show the buoys in relation to land and water marking points; the buoys are numbered to correspond with the charts.

Canal employee Edward J. Ahern checks buoy lanterns in March 1965 before they go out on the water. The lanterns were fueled with kerosene.
New York State Museum

Next, clusters of the red or green buoys are brought out onto the waterway, usually on the deck of one of the state's self-propelled derrick boats or scows. Today's plastic buoys are much lighter than the larger steel ones of earlier years. They are attached by a 20-foot-long cable to a concrete block that weighs 200 to 300 pounds. The buoys are set using the scow's crane.

At the end of the navigation season, the buoys are retrieved because winter ice conditions would quickly tear them from their moorings. In a reversal of the springtime activity, two crew members lean over the side of a scow and put the crane hook into the top of the buoy; the crane then lifts the buoy out of the water while another crew member guides it to the deck using a long hook. In the fall's cold and rainy weather, pulling the buoys can be a difficult and frustrating job. Sometimes the canalized rivers run so high that the boats are hindered from even reaching the buoys; the higher water makes the low canal bridges even lower, sometimes impassable. Sometimes the buoys are dragged by flood water to the shallows along the banks; a small tender then has to find the buoys and bring them to deeper water so the crane can pick them up.

In the fall of 1996, the *Ward's Island* and a crew of six picked buoys from Oneida and Cross Lakes and from the Oneida, Seneca, and Oswego Rivers as part of the normal end-of-season

The concrete buoy weights are removed from the lines which hold them to the buoys. The weights are collected on the deck of the *Ward's Island*. They weigh about 200 pounds each and are moved with the crane in the background.

Author's collection

The *Ward's Island*, now a self-propelled derrick boat, used to be a ferry boat to carry passengers from New York City to the state hospital on Ward's Island. This is the crew in 1964.

New York State Archives

activities. Early in the effort, the crew was challenged with swift, high water that completely covered some buoys. Some buoys were difficult to grab because the boat could not stay stable enough in the fast water to let the crew guide the crane's hook to the buoy. "When the buoys are bobbing around, we get them another time," captain Dennis Granley said about the swift current that fall.[6] A crew member remarked a few weeks later that with calmer water, "they ain't bent over," so that it would be relatively easy to pick the buoys up. "You can see 'em, you don't have to guess where they are."[7]

Granley recalled harrowing trips in other difficult years. "A storm caught us on Oneida Lake. We tried to outrun it but there was just a big whiteout. Then we just tried to see the buoys." In the fall of 1990, in high water, a buoy was caught by a dam at Lock 6 on the Oswego River. Three state canal workers in a 14-foot aluminum rowboat tried to rescue the buoy, but the boat's motor quit and the unforgiving current took the boat over the dam. Though two men jumped off before going over the dam, the other was swept over. Luckily, all survived.

The crew of the *Ward's Island* said that setting buoys in the spring was easier than pulling them in the fall. Years ago, setting the buoys still presented frustrations. The commercial boating firms wanted the canal open as early as possible, so the buoys sometimes were set and the canal opened prematurely. Ralph Folger, a retired canal floating plant supervisor, said, "We would open the canal for a week, then close it for a month because of high water. One spring we had to set the buoys five times."[8] A newspaper article from March 30, 1935, predicted an early opening. "Today's rain brightened hopes that ice in the Barge Canal will be cleared in time for the scheduled opening, April 8."[9] A March 26 article ten years later also looked forward to an early opening: "With Barge Canal traffic scheduled to open a week from today, state boats may attempt a crossing of Oneida Lake to determine the thickness of the ice and permit officials to schedule placing of channel buoys."[10] For the canal opening today (usually around May 1), colorful red and green buoys are lined up like soldiers on the decks of the state's work boats. It is a spring sight that means the canal will be ready soon.

About 30 of the more than 60 buoy boats that were built are still in operation. Each buoy boat is used to monitor about 75 miles of canal now. According to Geist, the monitoring is needed. People sometimes avoid using the canal because they fear hitting debris with their small wooden pleasure boats. "They shouldn't have to worry about that," he stated, remembering when the buoy tender could keep ahead of such problems."[11]

The next step up in the state's floating plant are the *tug tenders*. As the name implies, the boats were designed to perform light-duty tasks to assist tugs and other boats in the fleet. Their shallow draft makes them quite handy for several jobs, from bringing crews from the canal bank or quarter boat to the dredges, to pushing scows or pulling debris from the canal. The steel boats look like miniature tug boats. Many were acquired by the state in the 1920s; about 10 remain statewide. They take just a two-person crew to operate.

A much larger crew is needed to operate any of the Barge Canal *dredges*, the leviathans of the canal that are used to keep the channel deep enough for navigation. As with many of the state's canal craft, they are customized to the particular needs and dimensions of the canal. Some, in fact, though rebuilt several times, began with operating equipment dating back to the construction of the canal. The retired *Dipper Dredge Number Three* is an example. *DD-3* is basically just a big shovel mounted on a flat barge. It was originally known as the *Saint Johnsville* when it was built by a private contractor in 1910 for dredging the Mohawk River between Canajoharie and Little Falls. In 1918, the dredge

Tug tenders perform light duty tasks on the Barge Canal. This tender, built about 1925, is tied up in Syracuse Harbor about 1930.

New York State Museum (Scothon Collection)

reappears in the state's records as one of the machines enlisted to hasten the completion of the canal. The *Saint Johnsville* remained with the state after the Barge's completion; it was rebuilt in 1928 and 1929 and later given its current designation. Now resting at the state's Lyons dry dock, it is the last of the dipper dredges.

The four hydraulic dredges in the state's fleet range in age from the 1927 museum-quality *HD-3* to the relatively new *HD-1*. They operate like vacuum cleaners, sucking water and material from the bottom of the canal and running it through pipes that dump it beyond the banks of the waterway. They are most useful in removing fine silt that can be pumped easily into a settling basin (an upland spot surrounded by a dike). After the dredged material is put in the basin, the silt settles out and the water flows back into the canal.

Three long legs (called *spuds*) on the dredge—two in the front and one in the back—are used to keep the vessel steady while working. They extend down into the channel's bottom and provide the dredge with some ability to slowly move, crab-like, short distances. Normally, a tug or tender tows the dredge to a work site, since the dredge lacks traditional propulsion.

Derrick boats are another type of vessel used to keep the

A LONG HAUL

Above:
Just after the state's Waterford dry dock was put into use in 1925, these boats gathered there: two derrick boats, a tugboat and a tug tender. *The Chief* is still used by the state today.
New York State Museum (Scothon Collection)

canal's channels cleared. They use a huge clam shell to scoop material up from the bottom of the canal and put it in a dump scow (a flat, self-unloading barge with a large hold for collecting dredged material). Though they can work independently, sometimes a derrick boat and a hydraulic dredge support each other at the same site, the hydraulic dredge pumping away the spoils that are placed in front of it by the dump scow.

The *Ward's Island* is one of the state's more distinctive half-dozen derrick boats still in operation, its oddly rounded shape a reminder of its earlier life as a New York harbor ferry. (The boat was converted from a passenger ferry that shuttled between New York City and the state's hospital on Ward's Island.) It joined the state's fleet in 1937 after its upper housing was replaced by a crane. The crew uses the quarters below deck to fix meals and sleep occasionally when their job is far from home base. These days the crew has to bring food aboard, mostly for lunches. They recalled, however, in 1996 when they had to stay on the boat around the clock for five days and nights after the 1987 Thruway bridge collapse into Schoharie Creek. A lot of debris found its way to the Tribes Hill movable dam, immediately below the fallen bridge. The *Ward's Island* was needed to pull trees away

Opposite:
Top: This 1996 state crew of a tug tender monitors the pipe for a hydraulic dredge in the Champlain Canal.
Canal Society of New York State
Bottom: This derrick boat, the *Tenkanas,* at the entrance to Erie Barge Lock 10 in 1951, is a sister vessel to the *Ward's Island.* Also built in 1929 and acquired by the state in the late 1930s, it used to be a ferry boat, as well.
New York State Archives

from the dam during that holiday week. Another memorable event for the crew occurred when the boat's crane was used to clear debris one summer from the Mohawk River—they pulled up an old Plymouth from the river and the crew wondered if it had gotten there suspiciously. Sure enough, the car had the remains of a woman who had committed suicide by driving her car into the canal years earlier.[12]

A variant of the derrick boat is one canal workers refer to as the *gradall*, named after the manufacturer of its main working component. Instead of having a clam-shell scoop, the gradall has a rotating shovel on an extending arm mounted on the deck. With this capability it can efficiently reach the sloping sides of the canal.

A dredging operation often looks like a canal boat convention, with many blue-and-yellow boats milling around one spot. This is by necessity—the dredge has no living accommodations, like the tug has, and crews may not be able to conveniently go home every night. Housing needs are met by another vessel usually found at a dredging location—the *quarter boat*, a floating dormitory with sleeping, cooking, and limited bathroom facilities on board. The quarter boats were acquired or built by the state in the first decades of the Barge Canal. Only five remain on a roster that once listed nearly 20.

Ralph Folger remembered when the quarter boats had just a center sink with bunks all around the upper level. Eating facilities were below. When the dredge operated around the clock, the crews ate together on the quarter boat. And they ate well, according to the late Cal Pendergrass, chief lock operator at Erie Lock 17 and a former dredge hand. His father operated the steam-driven hydraulic dredge *General Herkimer* when the canal was being built, and he also took part in dredging the canal between Jacksonburg and Little Falls. Many years later the younger Pendergrass worked on a dredge. He later recalled, "You ate the best, and the state fed us good . . . anything you could imagine, just like you were eating at home. And Bucky Ladd, the captain, had a garden at home and all the vegetables and everything that he'd raise in his garden he'd bring along."[13]

In those days, accommodations on the quarter boat were cramped with the various shifts of full crews. There were 21 to 36 bunks on board, sometimes stacked three high. Crews worked 12-hour shifts; the dredge operated 24 hours a day. (The round-the-clock work was partly necessitated by the steam-driven equipment: It was time-consuming to shut down the fire and then restart it.) When two shifts were working, more than 30 workers

In 1962, this "canal boat convention" was actually a team of state boats working on the Champlain Canal in Whitehall below Champlain Canal Lock 12. *New York State Archives*

were needed, all living in close quarters and working hard for minimum pay. Former barge hand Bill Hills' comments about life generally on the canal in the 1930s are probably especially true when applied to life on the state's dredges: "It was a rugged business. They were a rugged people."

Another person who has known dredging first hand is Chuck Dwyer, of Sylvan Beach, recently retired from the state's canal force. Starting out on *DD-3* in 1946, he described the experience as "a job with three hearty meals a day." He was hired at age 16 by the captain as a courtesy to his father, a friend of the captain's. Recalling his low rank on the crew, Dwyer recounted that "the last one on the boat did everything," which gave him a not-always-welcomed taste of the various jobs on a dredge. The captain gave the orders for the day to the next rank below. "He didn't talk to me directly," Dwyer recalled. At slow times, Dwyer polished the brass and washed the windows. After doing that, if he still had nothing to do he was told to do it again.[14] One of the jobs he had was with the scows—he accompanied the dredged material in the scow when it was taken out into the lake and dumped. "There were no life preservers, and when it was windy the waves would wash right over you," he recalled. When the

Dump scows are the low-slung beasts of burden on the canal. They are barges designed to carry and dump material that has been dredged from the canal bottom. Here the state tug *Waterford*, built in 1950, is moving a scow along the canal in 1952.

New York State Archives

weather was really bad, he would ride it out in the ballast tank. Lunch was brought to the workers in a picnic basket via a rowboat from the quarter boat. The quarter boat was like an army barracks, "all opened up on the inside," Dwyer remembered.

After a stint in the navy, Dwyer chose to return to canal work in 1953 because, as he said, "I can get out and still have that feeling of being on water by being on the canal.")[15] Dwyer later became captain of *Hydraulic Dredge Number Three*.

Working with the dredges are the scows, the low-slung beasts of burden on the canal. *Dump scows* have a large hold for collecting debris scooped off the bottom of the canal and hinged bottoms that allow them to drop their loads in locations outside the navigable channel. *Flat scows* have a flat top used for carrying broken tree limbs, large lock parts, or other material. Both types of scows lack propulsion and are maneuvered by a tug or a tug tender.

The very versatile *self-propelled scows* are a notch up the design ladder in the canal fleet; they look like a scow but have an engine, cabin, and small crane. Their shallow draft enables them to reach farther into shallower areas to reach such potentially threatening debris as a downed tree. They also are often used in setting and pulling buoys. There are just over a half-dozen in the state's fleet.

The royalty of the canal fleet are the *tugboats*, vessels honored with names instead of numbers. Some are named to honor their performance, such as the *Urger* or *Reliable*. They are also named after great New Yorkers, like the *DeWitt Clinton* or the *Governor Roosevelt* and the *Governor Cleveland* (two nearly identical tugs obtained in 1928 from the Buffalo Marine Construction Company as icebreakers), or after canal communities, like the *Waterford*, the *Lockport*, and the *Pittsford*. Some of them were built by state workers—the sibling tugs *Reliable* and *Syracuse* were constructed at the Syracuse canal shops in the 1930s. Other boats were adapted from U. S. Navy surplus tugs. Most of the tugs began their lives as steam boats; all have since been converted to diesel, and all participate in the regular operations of keeping the canal's channels cleared and dredged.

The glory of the state's tugs is epitomized by the exploits of the tug *National*, now gone. The tug was specifically acquired by New York State to assist vessels in trouble on temperamental Oneida Lake. In the early days of the Barge Canal (when many of the older and vulnerable wooden barges were still used), tows were sometimes held up for days as crews waited for storms to clear on the lake. Many felt at the time that if the Barge Canal was a chain across the state, then Oneida Lake was its weakest link. For that reason, two tugs were assigned to protect vessels on the lake.

The state tug *National*, pictured here around 1936 at Sylvan Beach, was a rescue boat for the sometimes-dangerous Oneida Lake. It was built in 1918, acquired by the state in 1924 and sold in 1942. The captain, his wife and crew made perilous journeys out into the lake during storms to save boats and crews from destruction on the lake.

New York State Museum (Dwyer Collection)

A 1926 article in an Oneida newspaper gives testimony of one the *National's* adventures. It describes how the tug's valiant crew saved the steam canal boat *Brooklyn* and two others from wrecking near Verona Beach. "After being blown onto the sand reefs to the south of the canal entrance, the fleet was hauled to safety in one of the stormiest periods that the lake has seen this season."[16] The fleet was rescued after a busy day for the *National*. At noon the tug had helped two fleets of two tugs and eight barges to safety behind the Sylvan Beach concrete breakwater. "Shortly after 'chow', the crew was again called upon to face the dangers of the lake and a heavily rolling sea to bring the 'Transco Tug Number 5' and her fleet of five barges into port." At this point, *National* Captain Hubbard rescued the *Brooklyn* and her tow. "Working their way into the teeth of the gale and high seas, a line was thrown to the stranded fleet . . . Barge by barge, the stranded crafts were hauled from their sand perches and dragged into deeper water and as hawsers were taken up and the fleet reassembled the battle across the lake started. The 'National' accompanied the 'Brooklyn' and its tow as far as Cleveland, where the 'Brooklyn' signaled that all was well."[17]

The boats were saved from possible destruction on Verona Beach, a dangerous place, "the burying grounds of nearly 20 barges and tugs that have gone aground and been broken up by fall storms during the last three years."[18] Indeed, the *National* itself ran aground on the beach. Freed by a nearby dredge before any severe damage was done, the tug had only two weeks of respite before heading out again on a rescue.

"Buffeted by heavy seas for more than 12 hours when caught on Oneida Lake as a 50-mile-an-hour gale broke shortly after midnight Saturday, the 'Hedger' fleet with a crew of nine men and a $240,000 cargo of wheat, was rescued and towed to safety in Cleveland Harbor late Saturday afternoon." The *National* rescued the fleet "after braving the mountainous waves kicked up by high wind." The captain and crew of the *National* had volunteered to take the boat onto the lake before she had been fully serviced following her grounding on Sylvan Beach.[19]

When the *National* was beached in the earlier incident, she was trying to manage a fleet of barges that had broken from its tug, the *Walnero*. When all the barges became beached, it was very dangerous to maneuver around them because they started to break up from the action of the waves. Some local people in small boats came to the rescue, getting the crews of the *Walnero* and the barges back to shore. These local rescuers were Frank Dwyer and his sons, Melvin and Penthus. "The waves were rolling so high at the time the frail rowboat drifted toward the beach that the wreckage nearly thwarted the men in landing the rescued crews."[20] Frank Dwyer's grandson is Chuck Dwyer, the retired dredge captain mentioned earlier. He remembered, "The *National* had to go out in the worst weather," and, although he never worked on the boat, he remembered his mother, the tug's cook, telling him how scared she would be going out on the rescues—she could not swim.[21] The *National* was taken out of service when the number of wooden barges on the canal had been replaced by sturdier steel craft.[22]

Other state tugs with special duties are the steel-hulled ice breakers, the *Governor Roosevelt* and the *Governor Cleveland*. The state-built *Syracuse* also has pitched in with ice breaking, as it did during the sudden freeze of 1936, when almost 400 boats were frozen in the canal in early December. A contemporary account stated that "approximately 50 tugs and barges which had been at New London were freed by the state tug 'Syracuse' [and its] captain Jack Berney. This 250 horsepower craft pushed past the long string of stalled boats and opened a channel into Rome."[23] During that same freeze, the *Governor Roosevelt* was also in service and in the news: "The tug 'Roosevelt' has returned to Sylvan Beach to break the ice so as to try to get the buoys out of the lake. The tug 'Syracuse' stationed at the beach for that purpose was unable to get the buoys all in."[24] There were ample

The *Governor Cleveland*, seen here in 1939, was bought by New York State in 1928 as an ice-breaking tugboat. Along with its regular tugboat duties, this tug was equipped with a steel hull so that it could break ice through the channel in the late fall and early spring.

New York State Museum (Michon Collection)

Above:
The *Urger* is the flagship of the state's
canal fleet—it is the oldest tugboat still
in use in the state's fleet, although now
used just for educational programs.
Shown here in 1987 at Waterford, it was
built in 1901.   *New York State Museum*

Opposite:
Top: In 1987, this was the interior of the
Urger's pilot house.
                          New York State Museum.
Bottom: The *Urger* (on the left side of
this 1949 view) is dwarfed by the huge
motorships tied up below Erie Barge
Lock 3 in Waterford. The *Day
Peckinpaugh* is on the right in an earlier
version as the *Richard J. Barnes*. The
boats are tied up on both sides of the
canal like this to wait for the state to
repair a failed gate at Lock 5 on the
flight   *New York State Archives*

demonstrations at the time of how dangerous the ice could be.
An observer noted that "evidence of the pounding boats took as
they pushed their way through the ice . . . is seen on the copper
sheathing of the hull of the tug 'Maple Leaf' . . . It was cut, torn
and twisted in many places."[25]

Tugs have arrived in the state fleet in a number of ways. The
Urger, built in 1901, is one of the oldest operating tugs in the
nation. Now used for educational programs along the canal's
banks, it has worked for 64 years, pushing dredges, hauling scows,
and doing other maintenance activities. The *Urger* was first used
as a fishing boat on Lake Michigan, "an exceptionally well-built
vessel with considerable more power than was required for a fish
tug."[26] With so much power, the tug was used as a rescue craft on
the Great Lakes for the forerunner of the United States Coast
Guard. It came to the state fleet in 1922 and was retired from
heavy use in 1986. During that active life, her steam engine was
replaced with diesel, and the wooden structure on deck was
rebuilt in steel. What has not changed are delicate reminders of
her heritage, such as a bell system used to communicate with the

engine room. Since 1991 the *Urger* has been a traveling canal exhibit, allowing people a closeup view of a representative of the state's working Barge Canal.

The *DeWitt Clinton* is also one of the oldest tugs still working on the Barge Canal. Dating from 1925, it is one of the smaller tugs in the fleet and requires just a four-person crew.[27] The largest tug now working for the state is the *Grand Erie*, which joined the fleet in 1986 after use on the Allegheny and Ohio Rivers, and which looks more like a tour boat than a maintenance tug. In fact, the vessel is often used to escort officials and visitors on the inspections of the canal.

A victim of earlier cutbacks was an unusual craft in the fleet, the 75-foot yacht *Inspector II*. It was purchased in 1930 for use by Governor Franklin D. Roosevelt. One pundit noted, "He sailed her several times on the Barge Canal on what he laughingly described as 'official inspections' and maintained that the speeches along the way were 'non-political.'"[28] Roosevelt did visit many public institutions—army bases, hospitals, schools, prisons, and orphanages—using the *Inspector II* as his point of departure, and he also used the yacht to get a slow look at upstate New York to jump start his political campaign (some newspapers even referred to the boat as the "floating capitol").[29] At one stop at Three Rivers, a group of Democrats put on a fish fry in his honor on the banks of the canal. Roosevelt once took a swim from the boat in Oneida Lake, and a stop in Syracuse included a visit to the State College of Forestry on the Syracuse University campus.

Roosevelt began cruising the canal in 1928 on the state's first *Inspector*, the canal at that time just 10 years old. That first *Inspector* had been used in an official capacity since 1907 on the old Enlarged Erie Canal. Roosevelt wrote about these trips, "I would rather see [the natural beauties of the state] . . . while being seated . . . on the deck of a boat going along at a speed of six or seven miles an hour than I would from the most luxurious automobile ever made."[30] By 1930, the *Inspector* had aged, and its replacement, the *Inspector II*, was purchased. From then on, Roosevelt often traveled on the new yacht with an entourage that included the original *Inspector* for use by press and other officials.

Inspector II was the showpiece of the state's fleet—it had a rich, wood-grained interior, four staterooms, three bathrooms with full-sized tubs, and a glass-enclosed dining room and observation deck. Although succeeding governors did not use the boat nearly as much as FDR did, it continued to be used by legislators and public works officials for inspections. In 1960, Governor Nelson Rockefeller took it out of service to save money, and in 1963 it was

surplused. In private hands, it eventually ended up in Florida, where someone planned to make it into a floating restaurant. It was caught by the Coast Guard in 1980 illegally transporting 160 Cuban refugees to south Florida and sunk.

The state's fleet has regularly been observed from the side of the canal by other historic participants in the canal's operations: the *bankwatchers* who walk the banks of the canals every day checking for leaks in the land-line sections, especially in the western part of the state. (The canal there is often higher than the surrounding countryside, and catching leaks is critically important.) These bankwatchers, working when the canal is open, cover about seven miles of canal bank a day, first in one direction from their home port and the next day in the other direction.

Protecting the canal is what the state's floating plant does best. Whether saving boats in distress, dredging, or placing buoys, the Empire State's navy keeps the canal operating. This navy boasts a number of home ports, and although it is perhaps not as dramatic as an ocean-going fleet, it gets the job done and breathes historic character into the Barge Canal. The boats are reminders of the canal's days as a commercial highway. Though those commercial boats have mostly gone on, the hulking presence of the state's fleet of the same vintage speaks about that rugged era of waterway travel. The voices of the working Barge Canal are heard in the deep horn blasts of the tugs, the guardians of the water highway across New York State.

The state purchased the *Inspector II* in 1930 for $30,000. The 75-foot yacht, seen here in 1932, was used by Governor Franklin Roosevelt, who enjoyed seeing the state from this vantage point, as well as for inspections of the canal. It was taken out of service in 1960.   *New York State Archives*

7 Romancing the Canal

In 1939, a pair of newlyweds made their way across New York State on their canal barge, part of a tow carrying a load of grain from Buffalo. They crossed paths with two school teachers taking a vacation in a canoe. The barge captain, Herb Wilkins, asked the women, "Do you want to hitch a ride?" So the two teachers went along to learn a little about life on the barge. The captain's wife, Evamay Wilkins, offered them some tea and proudly brought them down into the cabin of the barge. As she later recollected, "I made 'em lunch and they admired the cabin because it was fixed up so pretty with little fancy curtains, like a young bride would do, and we had nice shiny linoleum on the floor." The teachers were admiring the bedroom when they noticed the marriage license hanging on the wall. "Oh Mary, they're married," one of the women said. Indignantly, Evamay Wilkins responded, "Of course we're married. You didn't think that I was one of these women that he picked up and . . ." She was proud of the new home that she had made with her new husband.[1]

Evamay Wilkins began her life on a canal boat in 1920 when she was just an infant. Her father's family (Mosseau) hailed from Cohoes on the old Erie Canal—her grandparents had a boat on the canal. Along with other siblings who were born during that time, she was on and off a canal barge with her parents during the 1920s. In 1930, in the midst of the Depression, it became too difficult for her father to support the family by working on the canal, so they moved ashore and lived in New York City for a number of years. Evamay returned to the canal in 1939 for two years with her husband—a childhood friend from another canaling family that also wintered their barge at Pier 6 in New York City.

In the years between Evamay's childhood and marriage the lives of canalers had changed. Her first experiences on the canal as a child were very similar to the experiences of a family on the nineteenth-century canal. The barge families of her childhood, however, had largely left the canal when she returned as a bride.

Opposite:
At the Rome Terminal around 1935, a cat captures the attention of a canal worker. *New York State Museum (Scothon Collection)*

By that time, canal boats, tugs, and barges were mainly operated by companies with nearly all-male hired crews.

Families sometimes had as many as 12 children, as Evamay recalled of neighbors on another barge. "They slept all over . . . Sometimes when they were real, real small we used to open up the big drawer and we'd put them in the drawer, so we'd know where they were. My mother would put 'em in the great big, big drawer that went into the wall. Everything was all built-in cabinets, built-in drawers."[2]

A reporter visiting a tow in 1935 described what "normal life" was like on a barge: "Whole families traveled on the Erie boats, even as they do today on the boats that ply the Barge Canal. Each boat had a cabin aft for the captain and his family and a bunk house forward of the hatches for the two or three hands. Clothes hung on a wash line, an ample, comfortable looking woman, obviously the captain's wife, sat in a rocking chair reading a motion picture magazine, a small child brown as a beach baby played with toys in the restricted area between the hatches and a white poodle lay in the sun."[3]

In contrast, the quiet could be shattered by a teenager in the next barge, as the article describes. "From another boat, when it was warped up to the dock, a young woman with blonde hair, red finger nails, a white sport costume and lips that had been bowed and reddened by a rouge stick, got off to take a walk until the barge was picked up by the tug on the other side of the lock. Before she left the boat, she turned off the radio in the cabin. In the winter she attends high school in New York and returns each night to the cabin of the boat, in which, as in summer, her family resides."[4]

Just like families on the nineteenth-century Erie Canal had adapted their lives to cramped canal quarters, so the Barge Canal families tried to remain conventional while carrying out mundane tasks on the deck of a barge. Like the stereotypical housewife on land, Evamay Wilkins listened to soap operas on the radio as she did her ironing; she always had a geranium on the top of the barge and her little white poodle to keep her company while her husband handled the barge. She learned to crochet and enjoyed that pastime when she was not at household chores.[5]

"It would take me all day to cook a meal because you had to cook on the coal stove [in the cabin]. I baked and cooked and sewed by hand. There was always somethin' to do."[6] (She admitted humorously that her baking efforts were not always successful. "When I burned the biscuits, I would just toss them

This woman, from the Huftill family photos, settles back in her chair on the deck of a barge. She's in Erie Basin in New York Harbor in about 1923.

Canal Society of New York State

into the canal." Her unknowing husband wondered why the flour was being used up so quickly.)

Doing laundry was a challenge on the barge. As canal families had done for generations (and as Wilkins did as a child and as a wife), water was taken out of the cleaner parts of rivers and lakes and put into washtubs. "We'd just leave the tubs out in the sun and when it got warm we did our washin'," Wilkins said.[7] Families also collected rainwater in barrels on the boat to use for laundry. The wash was hung on lines across the midship. Wilkins remembers a gale whipping up on Oneida Lake and blowing the laundry into the lake,[8] along with a baby carriage and other loose items on the deck. Canalers also filled drinking barrels from the lakes and from the hydrants in New York City—a piece of sulfur dropped in to keep the water fresh.

Herb Wilkins, a barge captain and Evamay's husband, sits on a coil of lines using a tin pail for a wash basin in the 1930s. *Evamay Wilkins*

The barge that Evamay Wilkins and her husband Herb lived on in 1939 was the *Mary F. Chapman*. Evamay fixed up the cabin with white curtains trimmed with a little red, and hung flowered drapes in the bedroom. The bed was pulled out each night from underneath the deck. Clothing was kept in built-in drawers because there was no room for a dresser. The kitchen had pots and pans hanging on the walls and a cook stove. The walls were covered with dark wood and wainscoting, and the white ceiling had exposed wooden beams.[9] She picked up one of the steps in the stairs to reach coal stored under there for cooking and heat.[10]

The *Mary F. Chapman* made a number of trips from New York harbor upstate while Evamay and Herb were aboard. In 1939, the barge carried sugar from New York to Rochester, and plaster and plasterboard from Rochester to New York (sometimes the boat went up to Rochester empty and returned with the plaster products). In 1940 the barge hauled sulfur from New York to Buffalo and iron ingots back to New York.[11]

The cargo hold served other purposes when Evamay was a child. In those earlier years (and probably for generations before), children of the barge families learned to take advantage of the room in the boat's hold. When the large midship was empty, she remembered roller skating and playing catch in it.[12] Her father put a swing made from scrap boat lines in the midship and also constructed a teeter-totter.[13] When the midship was filled with grain, her father let her and her siblings play in the open hold— as long as they were not caught by the grain inspectors.[14] Her brother, Joe Mosso, recalled trying to play in flaxseed stored midship: "It was so slippery, we just went right through," he laughed.[15]

More acceptable play areas were above. "We never played on the deck—it was always on top of the cabin . . . We always had the toys that my father made, tugs and barges . . . We always had an awning and a hammock."[16] The awning was set up on top of the cabin so they could play outside and be sheltered from the sun. When the boat was loaded, it sat low enough in the water so that the awning could be set up without worrying about low bridges. There were other worries, though. When her brother, Joe, was just about a year old he crawled up on the deck of the

A barge's midship, where the cargo was kept, was a great place for children to play when the hold was empty. The barge OCCO, new in this picture, was built in 1917 in Cohoes, and shows the empty cargo hold. In its lifetime it carried ore from Port Henry, wheat from the wést and then soda ash.

New York State Museum (Scothon Collection)

As a child, Evamay Wilkins and her siblings played on top of the barge cabin with toys her father made for them, like her brothers are doing here in the early 1920s. The wooden tugboat in her brother's hand was called *The Jumbo*.   *Evamay Wilkins*

barge and fell into the canal at Lock 17 at Little Falls, the deepest on the system. Her father dove into the water to save her brother.

Wilkins also remembered, "When we'd come to the lock my father would give us a chance . . . and we'd run . . . We always brought some flowers for my mother. We'd bring the dandelions down in the boat for her. And then my father would buy fresh milk off the farmer . . . and then my mother would make ice cream and have strawberry shortcake. And all the crew, all the other families, they'd all gather around our boat and we'd all have homemade ice cream . . . My father would play the harmonica and we'd sing."[17]

The late Austin Huftill was a child on his family's barge in the 1920s. Though born in Weedsport, he lived most of his life in Waterford. In a 1994 remembrance given at his Waterford home he quietly told of his family's experiences on the canal. Both his parents were raised on the canal—his mother drove teams on the Delaware and Hudson Canal as a youngster. Huftill, too, remembers playing on the top of the cabin (though his father tied a piece of rope around the son's middle so he would not fall off). Huftill played on swings rigged on the barge with leftover pieces of rope—"There was all kinds of rope on the boats," he said.[18]

Huftill did some painting and steering of the boat when he was young. "It wasn't too bad a life. You didn't know any better. The worst part was being confined to a small place," he said. "Every meal was a full meal with potatoes and meat," prepared in the small space of a barge's cabin.[19]

    A LONG HAUL

Being confined on the boat, Huftill also learned crocheting, embroidery, and tatting in the everyone-did-everything life on the barge. "Of course, you didn't do that in Brooklyn," Huftill remarked, referring to his winter school time on shore. "The kids there were talking about baseball—and I'd never played any baseball," he explained. His father taught him to crochet to help make the fenders for the protection of the family's boat. His on-shore schoolmates did not appreciate or try to understand the necessity of these seemingly girlish pursuits—they made fun of him when he demonstrated them as a school project.[20]

The Huftills, the Mosseaus, and the Wilkins were part of a community of canalers in New York harbor, where they tied up for the winter. Evamay Wilkins remembered gathering in winter at the Barge Canal terminal at Pier 6 on the East River of New York harbor with other barge families, the same ones each year. Their floating neighborhood, not unlike the more traditional on-shore neighborhoods, developed the same mutual support and friendship. All the boat children went to a nearby school, their life on the waterway sometimes envied by the other school children, according to Wilkins. Once the canal opened again in the spring the children would be back on the water and schooling would continue informally on the boats.

The children of Barge Canal families became friends when they tied up for the winter in New York Harbor and went to school. Here the children line up for a group shot on top of a barge. There are three families represented: the Pauquettes, the Costellos, and Evamay's family, the Mousseaus. Evamay Wilkins is fourth from left.
Evamay Wilkins

These canaling neighbors crossed paths on the canal during the navigation season and caught up on things while waiting for a lock. If they were in a tow together, people would walk from boat to boat to visit and play cards. "There was never no fighting, everybody was jolly," Wilkins recalled fondly of her childhood days on the canal. "There was always somebody who knew how to play the accordion or the guitar or the fiddle. And the families then . . . we'd get together and they'd sing. People would come down in the cabin, my father would recite these poems and tap dance. And we'd serve coffee and cake and it was always one big happy family. I just can't explain it. It was just wonderful, that's all."[21]

But there were times when money was tight and it was difficult for the family to make a living on the canal. One winter, Wilkins' father ran a gambling establishment on his barge while it was moored in New York harbor.[22] During Prohibition, he hid bootleg liquor from Canada to New York City among the legitimate cargo on his barge. His wife purchased the liquor on shore in Canada and used the family's baby carriage to bring it to the barge tied up nearby; they hid the stash under the floorboards in the barge's cabin. Wilkins recalled that as a child she was encouraged to use a chamber pot placed over a rug that covered the hiding place whenever prohibition inspectors came on the boat to search for smuggled liquor—they never disturbed her to check under the rug.[23] Her father sold the liquor to his friends once they got to New York harbor. (But, "It isn't like he sold oodles," she said.)[24]

It was still common in the 1920s to find barge hands bringing their families along on the canal journey because living costs were relatively low. Their needs were few (since they did not have to pay rent or worry about heat), and, even with few of the conveniences of life on shore, "When you were with your family, it didn't matter because it was your home," said the late Joe Mosso.[25] Mosso and his brothers must have found much in this canal life to like because they all stayed on the water through their working careers. As he explained in 1996 during one of his last trips as captain of the Hudson River tour boat, the *Spirit of Saint Joseph*, "At least we got something to eat."

But hauling on the canal was not steady work. According to Mosso, his father had to wait at a port and bid on jobs advertised in the paper. A group of barge families going the same direction would get together and hire a tug to pull them. The uncertainty extended to schooling when they were in port, he remembered. "We'd have this little pink slip to bring to school. We'd stay in school there until it was time for another run, then we'd leave."

Sometimes the barge operators got jobs through brokers, intermediaries who would know about jobs and line them up for the barge people. Sometimes, the profits they made by hauling were barely enough to scrape by with while they were tied up in port, but, "As long as you had enough money to eat, you are O.K. You don't have to pay for fuel or a house," Mosso said.[26]

Bill Hills, who worked on the water in 1936, offered another perspective of life on the barges. In December of that year he was dismayed when the canal quickly froze around his barge as it headed east from Sylvan Beach. He tried to continue with the tow through the ice, but only made it to the junction lock and harbor at Utica before his barge was frozen in solid. That year, 385 boats were stranded on the canal in the early, severe freeze. The state tugs were able to release 110 vessels, but the rest remained captured in the frozen water until spring.[27] Hills remembered that a tanker got through and that the tugs largely got out of the canal, but it was too risky for the wooden barges to try to break through the ice.

In the relative safety near the junction lock, Hills prepared to spend the winter on his barge, the *Mortimer B. Fuller*. The company that owned the barge paid him to stay on it all winter in order to break the ice day and night from around its wooden hull. (Without that daily work, the ice could easily damage the barge.) For that service, he was paid $52.50 per month. It was not

The *Dixie*, owned by the Hedger Transportation Company, is pulling some barges east out of Erie Barge Lock 12 around 1935. The *Dixie* was built in 1905 and scrapped in 1947. The stonework above its stern is the remains of a bridge abutment for a suspension bridge that crossed the river here before the Barge Canal was built.

New York State Archives

Above left:
The tugboat *Marmor*, built in 1905, pulled the barge tow that Bill Hills was a part of in 1936. This is a 1940 view of the boat below Erie Barge Lock 2 in Waterford.

Canal Society of New York State

Above right:
Bill Hills was a barge hand on the Barge Canal in 1936. In that year, his barge was frozen in the canal at the Utica junction lock. He spent part of the winter on his barge there and then switched to one at Lock 18 before Christmas. He revisited the site in 1995.

Author's collection

an awful winter, Hills remembered. His only personal expenses were for food and clothing; the company reimbursed him for the kerosene he needed for heat, and he did not need to be at the barge around the clock. Because the boat was out from the bank, he had to fashion a wooden plank to allow access to shore. He recalled going to the Stanley Theater in Utica to see a movie, for instance. Otherwise, "I shot the breeze with the other barge captains to kill time."

Later in the season Hills was able to switch boats with a barge captain on a boat that was frozen in near Jacksonburg's Lock 18—his father's barge was also stuck at that spot and Hills was thus able to be closer to him. They spent Christmas together on the barge, even celebrating with a small Christmas tree. During the rest of the winter, Hills spent time in the Little Falls community, attending church there and participating in a youth group.

Elmer F. Claire called his canal barge home during a 1958 interview with a newspaper reporter. His was the first barge in a tow of three barges hauling molasses pulled by the tug *F. A. Churchman*. From April to December he had a two-room apartment on the barge, "with no electricity and few of the amenities of modern life. His barge is a hulking steel tub 114 feet long, 38 feet wide and 14 feet high. It weighs 490 tons empty. In a center compartment for dry cargo it can hold 22,000 bushels of grain or 1,000 tons of pig iron. Surrounding this are liquid cargo tanks that can carry 1,000 tons of molasses."[28]

The length of Claire's entire tow was about 500 feet, so it had to be locked through in two shifts, called a *double locking*. The newspaper article explained that "the tug and one barge go through the lock first, leaving the other two barges tied near the

As a barge hand, Herb Wilkins operated the steering wheel on the back of the boat for eight-hour stretches. With the barges cabled together in a tow, the wheel used the cables to guide the tow.
Evamay Wilkins

lock entrance. Then the remaining barges are pulled into the locks by winches, lifted, and pulled out to rejoin the caravan. The process takes about an hour."[29]

The people on the tug of this 1958 tow worked 20 days in a row followed by 10 days off. They worked six hours on and then six off, around the clock. The tug had limited living arrangements. Four crew members slept in the cramped room toward the bow below deck; the four officers shared two small rooms on deck.

The commercial tugs were the bulldogs on the canal, pushing or pulling barges along. *Buffalo Evening News* reporter Ellen Taussig commented on the feel of a canal tug while traveling on the *Margot Moran* in 1967: "A tug is great power in a small package; it's really built around its engine and fuel tanks . . . When the tug is pushing along at a peak ten miles an hour, you feel pretty much as if you're sharing quarters with a chained panther. But you get used to it."[30]

A tug crew needed skill to approach and go through a lock: They had to avoid cross currents as the tow entered the chamber and gently bring the boats into a space not much larger than the

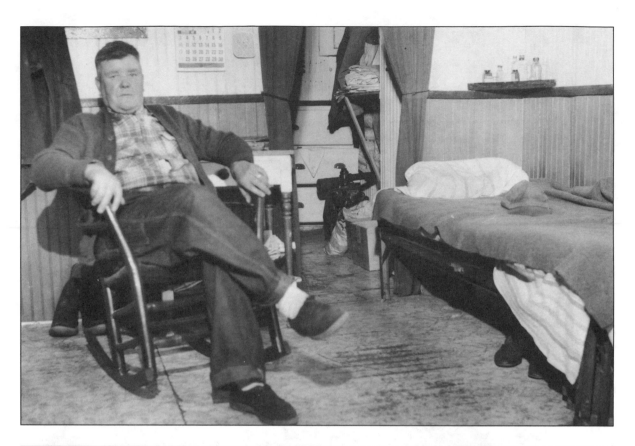

barge itself. But on the many long stretches between the locks crews often led a mundane life. Just as the barge families did, they had to make the tug seem somewhat like home. A summer's day might catch the crew doing wash in a bucket on the deck or touching up rusty spots with paint. Sometimes they just relaxed as they passed the time. Captain Chester "Chet" McDonald, with 23 years of piloting tugs behind him, recalled in 1966 what his work life had been like: "Being confined is the hardest part; we're hardly off the tug from port to port, and things can get a little boring. We've been slam-banged around on the lakes a few times, but all in all, the hardest part is waiting for those twenty days to be up."[31]

Home sometimes was glimpsed only briefly during those 20 days. McDonald said that during his shift he only saw his wife when she drove down to the lock to pick up the cook so he could get supplies.[32] (Evamay Wilkins also remembered meeting her husband at a lock and sitting in the car with him for a brief conversation before he had to return to the boat.)[33]

The crew had few chances to touch land during their 20 days unless it was necessary. "When supplies are low," McDonald explains, "our cook will jump off the barge at one lock, spend $200 off the top of his head at the nearest store, jump back

Opposite:
(Both photos): The cabin of the barge *Rose* in 1954 provided cozy, if cramped, living quarters. The barge was built in 1929.   *Canal Society of New York State (Gayer Collection)*

Below:
The *Frank Murphy*, built in 1928, is part of a tow leaving Erie Lock 10 in 1951. The barges looked like floating boxes. Living quarters were on the back of the boat; the entrance is visible in the center of this view, over the word "Frank."   *Canal Society of New York State*

aboard the next lock down with two week's grub, and never [be] more than $5 over his budget."[34] Tugboat cooks sometimes borrowed from another tug's kitchen. The 1967 newspaper article about the *Margot Moran* described how "community life goes on, too, as the cook of a neighboring tug, 'Seneca Chief,' comes aboard to borrow a loaf of bread."[35]

Many elements of tugboat life from the first days of the Barge Canal would be familiar to tug crews half a century later. Modern improvements on the tugs would have been gratefully received by those first Barge canalers. For instance, newer tugs had retractable pilot houses: When the tug approached a low bridge, the crew used a lever to lower the pilot house, raising it again after passing the bridge. The pilot house had to be high enough for the captain to see beyond the tow that the tug was pushing, but even then weather sometimes made it difficult to see where the tow was pushing. Radar was another improvement that made life on the tug easier and safer. "Ten miles an hour's our top speed, but we never stop, except for bad weather, and even then we try to keep going, using radar to 'see' the shoreline."[36]

Fred Godfrey, now of Fort Edward, spent more than 50 years on canal waters and experienced many of the changes in equipment and traffic. To his lifetime of canaling must be added his family's several generations of life and work on the Barge Canal (and on the Enlarged Erie before that). In his book of

The cook on the *James J. Murray* takes a break on the Waterford flight in July 1940. Tugboat cooks bought supplies at grocery stores in towns along the way.
Canal Society of New York State
(Michon Collection)

A LONG HAUL

recollections, *Sailors, Waterways and Tugboats*, Godfrey reviewed one of the bigger changes in tugboat life—the engines. In the 1920s, when as a youngster he helped his father on tugs, the vessels were steam-powered. The tugs stored a full load of coal on the side decks, ready to feed the boiler. The fireman in charge of shoveling the coal into the boiler was always busy trying to keep a good fire. Godfrey remembered the quietly distinctive sound of the steam tugs: "The slow turning of the old steam engines sent a rhythmic beat through the hull and gave a pleasant sensation for sleeping—like a baby rocked in cradle."[37] That characteristic rhythm of tug life was replaced by the more powerful but rougher diesel engine. Diesel engines meant that the crews could be smaller, since shoveling coal to stoke the boiler was no longer necessary, and tugs did not have to stop as frequently for fuel. Godfrey worked his first diesel tug in 1940. By the time he retired in the 1970s, nearly all tugs on the canal were diesel powered.

When a tug came to a lock, the horn blew three times to alert the lock operator to prepare the lock at any time, day or night. Godfrey remembered that during some early hours he would have to try hard to rouse a bleary operator. Godfrey, too, worked long hours—two weeks at a time—and he welcomed the

Here the crew of the *C. C. Brothers* takes a break in Erie Barge Lock 8 in June of 1940 to talk to a visiting family. This wooden tug was built in 1881 and later became the *Rose A. Feeney*.
New York State Archives (OSH Collection)

occasional evening at port. Despite the hard work (maybe because of it), he and many other canal retirees looked back positively over their years of service.

His family, too, had fond memories. Godfrey's uncle Frank, a dedicated canaler, married Daisy in 1911 when she was still in her teens. Also from a boating family, Daisy said, "I wanted to share my husband's life, and the only way I could go with him was to get my pilot's license."[38] There was a desperate need for tugboat captains during World War II, and Daisy became a member of an exclusive club, even for the canal—a female tugboat captain. She earned her title by studying navigation for five years and learning to read the water. "Then [with] her husband and sometimes her small son and daughter, she would ply the waters in their tugboat home, hauling iron ore and coal from Port Henry to Wilmington, New York to Philadelphia or Montreal," using the Barge Canal as a connector for many of the routes. "Sometimes we would be at sea for three months straight," she said. "I loved every minute of it."[39]

The Costello family also accumulated many years of memories on the canal. Now retired in Ticonderoga but formerly of Waterford, Nelson Costello was one of several brothers to follow in his father's footsteps on the canal. He got a job in 1933 with the crew of the motorship *Hartford SOCONY* (perhaps helped by the fact that his father was a former SOCONY captain). As an employee within the SOCONY network of oil-moving boats and tank farms, Costello was sent anywhere on the canal's connecting waterways, from the Great Lakes to Long Island Sound. On the *Hartford* he was one of a crew of 16 working three shifts a day.

These big tankers faced many challenges on the canal. The western section of the Erie—especially the 60-mile level between Rochester and Lockport—was always tedious. "We kicked mud from Baldwinsville to Buffalo," Costello recollected. Sometimes the heavily loaded ships would wedge or get stuck passing boats in the narrow confines of the western section. "Many times if we knew something was coming, we'd wait at one of the towns like Albion and kill an hour or two" until the other vessel passed, he recalled. (In later years the tankers were not needed on that end of the system because an oil refinery had been built in Buffalo and a pipeline carried the oil to Rochester and Syracuse.)[40]

One of the best-known canal families of all actually spent little time on the water. Two generations of Mattons built canal craft— first for the old canal above Waterford, then for the Barge Canal—at their Cohoes yard. Matton tugs were seen from New York harbor to every nook and cranny of the state's canal system

Opposite:
Top: SOCONY (Standard Oil Company of New York) had a number of tankers that delivered oil to upstate cities. The tankers were named after cities along the canal, such as this one, *Amsterdam SOCONY*, approaching Erie Lock 2. Probably taken on its maiden voyage, this view is from 1925.
New York State Museum (Scothon Collection)
Bottom: The Matton family ran a towing business and a boat building enterprise until 1964. Here the *Matton 10* is pushing an oil tanker about 1936.
New York State Archives

A LONG HAUL

during the Barge's peak commercial years. Ralph Folger, retired from the state fleet, worked for the Matton Company from January 1946 to June 1949 as an engineer on one of the Matton tugs, and he has fond memories of the company's operation and dedication. His experiences, however, date back to when he watched his father build boats at the Matton yard. He remembered that Mrs. Matton would still do her own grocery shopping long after she could afford to hire someone to do it for her, and the family always kept a hand in the nitty-gritty of boating operations, though they were rarely on the water. "The Mattons came from nothing," Folger recalled.[41]

Another common name on the canal, especially on its tugs, was Bushey. Joe Mosso worked for this Brooklyn-based tugboat company for decades. In the 1920s the Bushey company specialized in hauling fuel and it acquired tugs, barges, and terminals to handle the fuel. Mosso explained the well-recognized pattern of the names of the Bushey tugs: Most of the names started with a "Ch" and many of them drew on Native

Crew members on a barge, such as this pair on a barge in 1925, had to pitch in for all kinds of chores. They are washing the deck with a pail and a broom. The one holding the broom is Evamay Wilkins' father, William Mousseau.   *Evamay Wilkins*

American culture for inspiration—the *Chippewa*, the *Cheyenne*, and the *Cherokee*. The Bushey's *Chancellor*, now owned by the Oswego River Towing Company of Syracuse, is one of the last commercial tugs still afloat on the Barge Canal.

According to Mosso, the Busheys were at their busiest building tugs and other vessels during World War II (as were the Mattons). During the war, Bushey boats were painted an understated gray (their metal pilot houses previously had been painted and grained to look like wood). Some said, humorously, that the Bushey shipyard ended up with so much gray paint because of all its government war contracts, but many tugs, especially those working along the Atlantic coast, were painted that color to make them less noticeable to the wartime enemy. After the war, when the Bushey company was bought by Hess, the boats were painted a company green, like the company's gas station signs.[42]

Herb Wilkins worked for the Kehoe brothers, another Brooklyn-based, family-owned company that usually ran eight or nine tugs and a few barges. Wilkins was born on a barge under the Watervliet bridge and grew up as one of the Pier 6 kids. As an adult he worked on a number of Kehoe tugs, including the *Clayton Kehoe*, the *Martin Kehoe*, and the *George Kehoe*. According to Evamay, his wife, he was very loyal to Marty Kehoe. "He was willing to give up anything for him."[43] Loyalty from the

The crew of the *Dauntless No. 5* comes on deck while pushing a barge in Waterford about 1938.

New York State Museum (Michon Collection)

crews is what kept companies such as Kehoe afloat. Operating in stiff competition, Kehoe was able to get enough business to keep operating years after several of his competitors had gone out of business.[44] Wilkins died in 1969 while on a Kehoe tug just at the end of the shipping season.

These family tugboat businesses invited generations to continue on the tugs. In *Low Bridges and High Water*, by Charles T. O'Malley, the sometimes colorful struggles of these enterprises is well described. A particularly good example is offered by the history of the Coyne family of Syracuse. The family was unusual in that it had just one boat for a number of years, the *Thomas R*. There was little time off for the crew, made up of mostly family members, but nevertheless the family decided to expand the company with the purchase of another boat in 1935, a U. S. Navy tug built in 1919.[45] Frank, the father, renamed the wooden tug the *Coyne Sisters*. Along with service on the canal, he used her for disaster service following the hurricane of 1938, when he towed damaged boats into Long Island Sound for demolition.[46]

Frank Coyne and the family primarily hauled oil until their shipping contract with Sears of Utica expired in the mid-1940s. The next decade was not good; the Coynes were only able to take a few odd jobs such as moving barges for a construction company. The family moved off the tug and got jobs elsewhere: One son, Tom, went to work on one of the state's dipper dredges; another son, Joe, went into selling real estate. They had to sell the *Thomas R*. in 1953. The family pushed oil barges again from 1955 to 1958 with the *Coyne Sisters*, and some of the children ended up back on the tug.

Tom Coyne did not fit the usual description of a tugboat man as O'Malley describes—he tended to be a bit more distracted than his single-minded parents when it came to canal work, and once even stopped the tow to pick water lilies.[47] An observer noted, "There is something unique about [his] vessel, for in addition to the grain, oil and other cargo he delivers, 'Captain Tom' carries Bibles in his cabin and watches for opportunities to place them in the hands of those who are without Scriptures."[48] Coyne's unusual diversion originated when, years earlier, someone made an impression on him by similarly giving him a Bible. "He was on his father's tug, anchored in New York Harbor, when an elderly man rowed out to the boat, and without coming aboard, handed a Bible to the lad [Tom] standing at the gunwale . . . Many people around canal depots, in the harbors and on the crews of other boats have had the opportunity to possess the Scriptures through the work of 'Captain Tom.'"[49]

The *Coyne Sisters* was taken off the canal in 1958 and the family once again got jobs ashore. The *Coyne Sisters*, sold in 1968 for a dollar, sank twice at the hands of different owners. Eventually, left grounded in Syracuse harbor, she was taken apart and discarded, the last commercial wooden tug on the Barge Canal.[50] The iron bits from the tug are now in the flower garden entrance to the Barge Canal shop at Syracuse.

The cargoes that these canaling families depended on have now all but disappeared. Some firms, such as the family-based Moran Towing, were more successful through this transition because they didn't specialize in canal work but focused on towing jobs year round in New York harbor. The current commercial traffic on the Barge could not keep even a single towing business going.

Today's pleasure boaters tie up at the dock walls where once the commercial tugs and barges snubbed up. The new boaters are not on the canal to make money but to enjoy the water and experience the vistas of upstate New York. The people on these boats also live in small quarters, but only for recreation; they stop when and where they like, not according to the demands of commercial cargoes. They can stop at a lock or a marina, visit

The *Nadia Des Rosiers*, the barge in the foreground of this c.1930 photo, was built in July 1927 and sunk in June 1931 after colliding with the motorship *Clevelander* at Little Falls. Barge families would look forward to docking here at Sylvan Beach, where there was an amusement park and other diversions. Boats also tended to collect here while waiting to cross Oneida Lake if the weather on the lake was bad. Notice the Sylvan Beach weather tower in the background.
New York State Museum (Everhart Collection)

restaurants, historic sites, or even sleep overnight in a nearby hotel. Most of the people they see on other boats are strangers who they welcome with a wave. Their friends are usually elsewhere; their community is back at home. For them the canal is an extra, not a necessity. They are drawn to it.

Many of the state's new canalers got their first experience of the canal on a Mid-Lakes Navigation tour boat. This Skaneateles company was started in 1968 by Peter Wiles, who had developed a vision for the Barge Canal around which his company grew. Wiles fought for the canal in the early 1970s with an "acquired passion," his son, Dan, says. His crusade was "Don't close it!" His words came at a time when the very existence of the canal (at least the western end), was in jeopardy because of the decline in commercial traffic. "Dad thought the western end was the best part—more ditch-like, through quiet villages. He said that if

In 1951, when this photo was taken, the Barge Canal carried over 5 million tons of cargo, its peak year. At that time, oil tankers, such as this one at Erie Barge Lock 2 in Waterford, shared the canal with pleasure boats. Now the commercial boats are largely gone.

New York State Archives

A LONG HAUL

they closed it, they would never open it back up and we would lose that heritage."[51]

Wiles fell into canaling when he expanded a dinner-cruise business he had on Skaneateles Lake. One day he brought his cruise boat to the Rochester area to give tours to some school children and saw the potential of the canal. "He was very hungry, going wherever the money was," Dan Wiles says of his late father's effort to build a tourism market on the Barge Canal. By the mid-1970s the company offered regular canal cruises at a time when many people were turning away from the canal. "Our trailblazing efforts have led to the others," Dan says, referring to the other tour companies that have started on the canal since.[52] The company expanded into the boat-rental business in the 1980s when Peter traveled to Europe and saw the way the Europeans enjoyed, preserved, and even resurrected their canals. A tenacious businessperson, he realized that the Barge had no such convenient rental business, so he decided to start a rental operation.

Since the 1995 death of Peter Wiles, his wife and five children have been carrying on these new canaling traditions. Dan traveled on the canal with his father when the cruise boat shared the waterway with the last of the commercial traffic. He

Tour boats like the *Emita II* from Mid-Lakes Navigation Company introduce a new generation of canalers to the Barge Canal, in this case the author's children at Lock 32 in 1995.   *Author's photo*

remembers hearing the barge in front of their boat call ahead on the radio to order groceries at the next stop. The state's last dipper dredge was still operating then, and he said that it looked like a dragon working. He mourns the loss of the drawbridge on the Oswego Canal, and of the bells at the lift bridges that signaled when the bridge was being raised. According to Dan, his appreciation for the historic and natural beauty of the canal is a direct result of his father's influence.[53]

Sue and Bill Orzell of Syracuse began their canal interest when they were trying to learn more about the DeRuyter Reservoir, a water source for the canal, where they have a summer camp. Their passion to learn all about this nineteenth-century reservoir turned into a passion for the canal and all its inner workings. Soon they were exploring the placid waters of the canal itself in their small pleasure boat. "It's very pastoral . . . You pass slowly through rural country." Earnestly, Bill adds that it was "neat to see all the locks and bridges and realize that they had been operating since 1918."[54]

The Orzells enjoyed discovering remains of the old Erie Canal and looking for small towns to experience on their weekends and brief summer journeys on the canal. As Sue states, "We try to stop every night at a different little town." They like to eat out at local restaurants—especially the one where "some guy comes down to the lock and gets you in a car to go to the restaurant. We have offered to walk back to the lock after dinner, but he won't hear of it."[55] Some other favorite spots are Fairport and Oswego, where the towns have geared up to attract boaters.

When they first started making trips on the Barge Canal in 1987, the Orzells looked forward to crossing paths with what little commercial traffic that was still operating. "You could practically smell the asphalt barge long before you could see it," they said of the commercial tug *Morania*'s barge of hot asphalt bound for Lyons from New Jersey.[56]

These large barges were at times difficult to share the canal with, and the Orzells remembered one incident vividly. "When the *Mobil Champlain* barge was on strike, it was operating with a scab crew," Bill says of the non-union replacement workers. The boat was carrying jet fuel and striking workers had threatened to blow up the tanker in one of the locks. The barge approached Lock 4 on the Champlain Canal and came upon the Orzells, who had their small boat just outside the lock for the night, with permission from the lock operator. The crew of the *Mobil Champlain*, though, was suspicious and decided to harass the Orzells, thinking they were strikers—they revved the motors of

the much-bigger boat so that their small boat was sucked away from the side and toward the middle of the canal. "I had to jump into the water in my pajamas and pull on the lines to keep the boat into shore. They shone big floodlights on us, too," Bill recollects.[57] The crew eventually realized their mistake and moved on.

Most of the Orzell's trips are not that exciting, usually only punctuated by the clack of the gears turning as the lock gates open and by the conversation of boaters they come across. "Most of the boaters we meet are just passing through the canal on their way from the Atlantic to the Great Lakes. We met one couple that had come all the way from Belgium." (Sue added, "The way they were arguing trying to get the boat in the lock, I don't know how they made it all the way across the Atlantic.")[58] On one trip, the Orzells came across a lock full of dead fish (probably herrings). The sea gulls diving after the fish made it a miserable time to be in the lock.

Nonetheless, the peaceful beauty and historic nature of the waterway appeal to many like the Orzells, though to them, "Summer's too short on the canal."[59]

This pleasure boat shares space on the canal with an oil tanker in 1962, looking south at Champlain Canal Lock 11.
New York State Archives

Page 171:
In 1936, the canal froze early, catching long lines of wooden barges in the canal. People were hired to stay on the barges all winter and break the ice around individual barges so the wooden sides would not get damaged. This line of barges was trapped east of Sylvan Beach.
New York State Thruway, Canal Corporation

The Year the Canal Froze Early

On November 15, 1936, a cold snap caught upstate New York in its icy grasp for an entire month. The Barge Canal was still open, and it was quite busy as boats started into their final trips before the canal closed for the season. The New York State Department of Public Works had purchased two ice-breaking tugs, the *Governor Roosevelt* and the *Governor Cleveland*, in 1927 just for times like this, but the severity of the freeze soon overwhelmed even their capabilities.

Everyone was caught by surprise: The freeze happened fast and the boat-stopping ice became thicker daily. Even the large SOCONY oil barges were trapped by the quick-forming ice, as were almost 400 wooden tugs, barges, and some other steel tankers and tugs. Harvey O. Schermerhorn, state commissioner of canals at the time, said the freeze was "probably the worst tie up in the canal's history."[60] By December 2, canal traffic in central New York was at a complete standstill in ice varying from four to six inches thick.

Crews of the tugs and barges tried everything they could to get out of the canal because the companies they were hauling for would lose money if the loads were left in the canal all winter. Schermerhorn said the 175,000 tons of trapped cargo—mostly wheat, pig iron, and oil—was worth about $10 million.

The boats stranded on Oneida Lake were in the most difficult position. A newspaper reported that "with food and fuel provisions dwindling, 70 men aboard five stranded motorships" on the lake were hoping the wind would change direction and move the ice floes around and allow them to escape.

But the ice was 18 to 20 inches thick and the only way to reach the ships—about 2.5 miles from shore, was by airplane. "Quarters of the mighty vessels are well heated, and their only worry is the food and fuel supply."[61]

Between Rome and Sylvan Beach there were 49 barges, 2 tankers and 12 tugs. A report of December 3, 1936, stated that "with arrival of additional fleets, Sylvan Beach Harbor is 'filled to the limit', a condition which local residents have never seen before. General stores and hotels open during the winter reported a 'landoffice' business from early morning until closing hour."[62] The 1,000-ton tanker *Transoil* and the state tugs *Seneca* and *Syracuse* were breaking a channel through the ice to let the boats stuck in Sylvan Beach get to Rome, where the facilities were better. (The ice was a foot thick in some parts of that section.) Water was released from the Delta Reservoir with the hope that raising and lowering the water levels would help break up the ice.

The tug captains became worried that their coal supplies would run low—they had expected to refuel under normal conditions but the freeze prevented them from reaching coaling points. Additionally, they needed to keep their boilers well stoked and ready to go in case the ice broke enough to allow a momentary opportunity to head east. "They may be marooned until spring," Schermerhorn stated, "unless a week of warm weather saves the day."[63] Some barge captains worked valiantly to break their crafts free, while others accepted philosophically the prospect of a winter in upstate New York. The barge crews explained to a Syracuse newspaper reporter that a winter-long

assignment on the canal would be necessary for some in order to guard the boats and their loads. "They live aboard, keeping a generous supply of dynamite on hand for breaking out ice when its pressure threatens to damage the boats."[64]

At the end of the year, the New York State Department of Public Works reported that it had been able to get out just 110 vessels of the 385 initially stuck in the ice.[65] The rest were not released by the upstate snow and ice until the following spring.

8 Business and Beyond

The colorful, shiny, fiberglass yachts and motorboats traveling on the canal today are a far cry from what the canal planners had in mind when the wide waterway was conceived. They saw it as a lifeline for farms and factories within and outside New York State on which to receive raw materials and ship out their products. The canal was to confirm the "commercial supremacy" of New York State, according the state's Committee on Canals in 1899. It was also seen as a way to win back the grain trade that New York was losing to other shipping avenues and to help develop the iron and steel industry in the state.[1]

Commercial supremacy was a noble goal, but it was not reached through the Barge Canal. However, the canal did carry products in large enough quantities to make an impact on the state's economy: Grain from Great Lakes ports went east, as did paper from Canada and agricultural products such as corn; shipments going west included oil from storage facilities in Albany, scrap iron and molasses to Buffalo, chemicals and fertilizer for agricultural needs in the West, iron ore from the Adirondacks, casting sand from New Jersey to the foundries of Utica, and sugar from Cuba. Some materials, such as fuel oil, were shipped for most of the commercial life of the canal; other products were shipped for just a short time, such as sugar, which was on the canal in large amounts only from about 1927 to 1940.

In 1917, a year before the Barge was completed, New York State Superintendent of Public Works William Wotherspoon predicted the commercial successes of the venture: "If economy in freight movement is desired, the canals will supply it. If a prompt and speedy receipt is demanded, the waterway at the present time excels the railroads. Whatever may have been the performance of the railroads in other times, it is a matter that may be proved beyond doubt that cargoes by canal pass from Buffalo to New York in less time than by rail. Already, with a portion of the old canal in use and by means of antiquated canal boats, a fleet has made the trip from the Great Lakes to New York

Opposite:
This steel fleet is entering Crescent Lake from the top of the Waterford flight in 1922. The tugboat pulling the five barges is already in the lake. The barges were built by the federal government in World War I.

New York State Archives

in a little more than seven days. With the new canal route in use for its entire length, five days may be counted as the maximum time of passage."[2]

When the canal opened, people were pleased with the new equipment and wider waterway, even though shippers were still using outdated boats built for the Enlarged Erie Canal. Loads were very small compared to what the new canal could handle, but with so many boats the canal still carried over a million tons in 1918.

Traffic on all canals[3]

YEAR	TONS	YEAR	TONS	YEAR	TONS
1900	3,345,941	1932	3,643,433	1964	3,194,696
1901	3,420,613	1933	4,074,002	1965	3,270,796
1902	3,274,610	1934	4,142,728	1966	3,147,129
1903	3,615,385	1935	4,489,172	1967	3,219,994
1904	3,138,547	1936	5,014,206	1968	3,249,035
1905	3,226,896	1937	5,010,464	1969	3,248,440
1906	3,540,907	1938	4,709,488	1970	2,734,963
1907	3,407,914	1939	4,689,037	1971	2,488,205
1908	3,051,877	1940	4,768,160	1972	2,509,069
1909	3,116,536	1941	4,503,059	1973	2,548,113
1910	3,073,412	1942	3,539,101	1974	2,222,827
1911	3,097,068	1943	2,824,160	1975	1,940,772
1912	2,606,116	1944	2,506,840	1976	2,227,052
1913	2,602,035	1945	2,968,682	1977	1,826,878
1914	2,080,850	1946	2,820,541	1978	1,553,310
1915	1,858,114	1947	3,790,050	1979	1,303,337
1916	1,625,050	1948	4,513,817	1980	1,148,382
1917	1,297,225	1949	3,949,739	1981	807,925
1918	1,159,270	1950	4,615,613	1982	777,292
1919	1,238,844	1951	5,211,472	1983	579,777
1920	1,421,434	1952	4,487,858	1984	457,134
1921	1,270,407	1953	4,497,231	1985	401,132
1922	1,873,434	1954	3,859,335	1986	373,950
1923	2,006,284	1955	4,616,399	1987	398,313
1924	2,032,317	1956	4,858,044	1988	415,665
1925	2,344,013	1957	4,468,539	1989	345,735
1926	2,369,367	1958	4,000,580	1990	263,055
1927	2,581,892	1959	3,719,919	1991	213,830
1928	3,089,998	1960	3,415,095	1992	162,349
1929	2,876,160	1961	3,223,558	1993	153,640
1930	3,605,457	1962	3,279,944	1994	67,783
1931	3,722,012	1963	3,225,526	1995	21,789

In 1924, when the canal's commerce picked up significantly, there were 877 commercial boats registered for use on the canal, most of them wooden barges carrying from 300 to 500 tons.[4] Ten years later there were fewer commercial boats—just 736—but those boats carried more than twice the tonnage. The canal was getting more efficient as a freight hauler. By 1936, the state reported that the "increasing use of motorships and of large single steel barges" was making it easier for vessels to get through the canal quickly, and, of course, to carry larger loads in one trip.[5]

By 1948, the fuel oil to heat many homes in the canal corridor counties was provided by five suppliers who used only the canal to move their shipments.[6] Oil was shipped in the largest quantity of any item over the life of the Barge Canal.

Clearly, though, Barge Canal planners had thought that grain would constitute the bulk of the canal's commerce. As early as 1874 a United States Senate committee reported that "the western grain regions were directly interested in the development, the improvement and the maintenance of" the Erie Canal. The canal's position as a regulator of railroad freight charges on grain was deemed to be of "supreme importance" by the committee.[7] Indeed, shipments of wheat, corn, oats, rye, and

The Barge Canal was a lifeline for factories both within and outside New York. The motorship *Robert Barnes Fiertz*, a sister ship to the *Day Peckinpaugh* (originally the *Richard J. Barnes*), was built in 1921 and hauled general bulk commodities. Here it is entering Lock 10 on the Mohawk River in December 1951.

New York State Archives

Above:
Shown by this c.1940 view, the Harbor Tow Boatmen's Union Hall was regularly visited by many a canaler on the Waterford waterfront. The union represented the individual worker on the water for employment and protection in dealing with the towing companies.

New York State Museum (Michon Collection)

Opposite:
Top: This hoodledasher leaving Erie Barge Lock 2 around 1938 was a style of boat that combined barge and tugboat. The *J. R. Hutton* was built in 1914 and sunk in 1947. *Canal Society of New York State*
Bottom: The *Carutica* was part of the Cargill fleet of grain barges with separate propulsion units. The high, box-like unit in the back of the barge could come off and be attached to another combination of barge units. This view is below Erie Barge Lock 2 in Waterford in May 1953.

*Canal Society of New York State
(Gayer Collection)*

barley increased steadily during the first years of the Barge Canal, and the sight of a grain boat on the canal became very common. In 1918, the total grain shipment on the canal was just 60,297 tons; by 1931, it had peaked at 1,209,480 tons.[8] In 1921, a Rome newspaper remarked, "Grain-laden barges are traveling east on the Barge Canal, more than 100 of them carrying 50,000 bushels each, going through Rome this week."[9] Wheat accounted for about 75 percent of the total tonnage of grain traffic.

The grain shipments steadily declined after 1931 for many reasons. The railroads lowered their rates and captured more of the grain traffic. An enlarged Welland Canal in Canada offered an alternative route through the Great Lakes to the St. Lawrence River. The Depression in the 1930s inspired European countries to protect their own farmers by imposing higher tariffs on United States wheat. Additionally, the Soviet Union was improving its farm production and thus importing less. A decade later, war-crippled Europe reversed some of these trends and export grain traffic increased on the canal; even more wheat was shipped to a recovering Europe in the late 1940s under the Marshall Plan. In 1948 the largest single load of wheat ever to move on the canal up to that time cleared Oswego—3,267 tons on a Cargill barge.

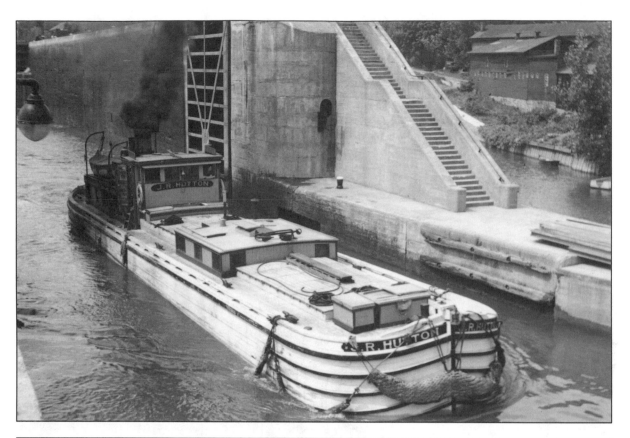

The growth spurt, however, did not continue. Government-sponsored shipments to Europe were reduced in 1950, and wheat traffic on the canal dropped by half a million tons.[10] The next big decline came with the opening of the St. Lawrence Seaway in 1959—by the end of that year, the movement of wheat on the canal had been almost completely diverted to the new Seaway.[11]

Originally, most of the canal's grain moved through Buffalo eastward to New York City. Not until 1932 did substantial amounts enter the system via the Great Lakes at Oswego, when the state's superintendent of public works reported that "for the first time in its history, there has been some real business at the Oswego Grain Elevator."[12] This was an indicator of the new route that grain was taking through Lakes Erie and Ontario by way of the just-enlarged Welland Canal connecting the lakes. By 1949, 92 percent of the canal's grain moved from Oswego to Albany.[13]

Recognizing this new avenue, in 1929 the United States Army Chief of Engineers called for improvements to the Barge Canal.

The dredge *Baltimore* is working on the federal improvement project west of Rome in this 1937 view. The project widened and deepened the canal and raised bridges, but it was not completed until the 1960s.

New York State Thruway, Canal Corporation

A LONG HAUL

This pair of SOCONY barges, built in 1921, is pulled by a steam tugboat in November 1923 in Pittsford. SOCONY also used much larger self-propelled motorships to transport oil on the canal.

New York State Museum (Scothon Collection)

(The federal government justified the improvement project because of its responsibility to develop and maintain the navigable waterways of the United States for economic growth and national defense.) In May 1935, Congress authorized deepening the canal to Oswego to 14 feet generally, with a 13-foot depth over the sills of the locks; bridges were raised to allow a minimum 20-foot clearance, and the bottom of the canal was widened. The 30 locks between the Hudson and Oswego were affected and 56 bridges raised; more than 183 miles of channel were deepened or widened. The channel deepening was not finished until 1963; the bridge-raising project was concluded a few years later.

Grain's preeminent position as a commodity on the Barge eventually was overshadowed by oil. They both showed steady growth through the 1920s—grain peaked in 1931 with about 1.2 million tons moving on the canal, then slipped back. Petroleum shipments, though, continued to climb: In 1951, almost 4 million tons (29.8 million barrels) of petroleum were shipped on the canal, compared to just 665,339 tons of grain.[14] It became much more common to see a petroleum barge than a grain barge by the 1940s.

The ships carrying petroleum picked up their loads in either Albany or New York harbor. They took it to 45 different cities and villages in New York State and also to ports outside the state,

Where was the oil going in 1949?[17]

	TONS	%
NEW YORK STATE		
Utica Area		
(incl. Rome)	554,120	25.00
Rochester	353,366	15.94
Buffalo Area	285,205	12.87
Syracuse	256,682	11.59
Plattsburgh	113,930	5.14
Ogdensburg	73,936	3.34
Schenectady	63,927	2.89
Subtotal	1,701,166	76.77
Misc. New York terminals		
	516,402	23.23
NEW YORK STATE TOTAL		
	2,217,568	100.00
OTHER U. S. CITIES		
Burlington, VT	257,507	66.00
Detroit, MI	42,204	10.82
Toledo, OH	21,297	5.47
Trenton, MI	20,114	5.16
Misc.U. S. terminals		
	48,914	12.55
OTHER US CITIES TOTAL		
	390,036	100.00
CANADIAN CITIES		
Toronto	67,709	75.18
Misc.Canadian terminals		
	22,341	24.82
CANADIAN CITIES TOTAL		
	90,050	100.00

such as Burlington, Vermont, and to Canada. Most of the shipments went to Utica, Rochester, Syracuse, and Buffalo.[15] At these bigger cities, companies established storage facilities known as *tank farms*—the wide, squat silos held enough petroleum to get these communities through the winter months when the canal was closed. Forty-one counties in New York State depended on the Barge Canal as their primary source of petroleum by 1948, and almost all of the kerosene used in the state was transported by canal.[16]

In 1949, 25 companies operated oil barges on the Barge Canal. Ninety to 100 barges and about 27 tankers delivered oil to upstate cities and villages.[18] The *Mobil Champlain* and the *Syracuse Sears* became familiar sights to those who watched the waterway in those active years.

The late Joe Mosso worked on the canal for nearly 50 years and recalled when the oil barge traffic was heavy. "The company [Bushey] would bid on fuel runs for a year and it would give us steady runs. We would carry 15,000 barrels of oil and stop, say, in Amsterdam to drop 5,000, then in Utica another 5,000 barrels, and then in Rochester. I remember when there'd be five or six oil barges tied up at the Mobil terminal at the Port of Albany."[19]

The Standard Oil Company was one of the first companies on the scene when the Barge Canal opened. In 1920, the nine tank barges in its Barge Canal fleet each were able to hold about 200,000 gallons. That year the company built five self-propelled barges that would each hold 700,000 gallons. The company also bought property along the shores of the canal in many cities to establish storage facilities—the harbor and dock in Rochester alone cost Standard Oil $100,000 in 1920, part of the millions of dollars in property and equipment the company invested that year. The state's superintendent of public works used the company's activities as proof that people would invest in the canal as they discovered that water transportation was indeed more efficient.[20]

By 1961, huge barges that could carry over 800,000 gallons of petroleum appeared on the canal. Commenting on a Utica-based company, a reporter noted that "the twin barges, named the 'Albany Sears' and the 'Syracuse Sears' each have a capacity of 19,500 barrels, or 810,000 gallons, of petroleum products. Never before [had] the canal carried such giants."[21] Sears barges used an innovative design—the stern of the barge had a V-shaped notch that allowed the tug pushing to fit into the rear of the barge, which meant that it took up less room in the lock so more space could be devoted to cargo. It also gave the tug more control when steering the barge, especially around bends in the

This oil barge fills Lock 9 on the
Champlain Canal in 1962.

New York State Archives

channel. These Sears barges were 230 feet long and 42 feet wide.
Twelve separate compartments held the petroleum, and a steam
circulating system kept the oil warm so it would not congeal.
There were separate quarters for the captain and the two mates,
who were responsible for loading and unloading the barge and
for general maintenance.[22]

These large barges received their loads in Albany, a deep-water
port. Its 27-foot depth (later increased to 32 feet) allowed ocean-
going tankers to come from New York up the Hudson River. The
petroleum was transshipped from the ocean-going ships to storage
tanks to canal barges in Albany, then distributed to terminals in
Utica, Rome, and Syracuse. The barges made 35 to 40 round
trips a season and took about 8 to 10 hours to unload.[23]

Petroleum also accounted for most of the traffic on the
Champlain Canal, much of it going north from Albany to the
United States Air Force base at Plattsburgh and to the city of
Burlington. The canal's importance as a fuel-delivery route was
demonstrated when Burlington officials once called Joseph
Stellato, then director of operations for the Barge Canal System, to
see if the canal could open early because the city's winter fuel
supplies were getting low. By 1971, tonnage carried on the

Champlain Canal amounted to more than half of what was carried on the entire system—thanks to petroleum shipments to the air force base. Petroleum also was barged to a storage facility on the banks of the Barge Canal at Rome for Griffiss Air Force Base.

Petroleum barges also carried more than what was expected during World War II because of German submarine activity along the Atlantic seaboard: Oil from the Gulf Coast, which normally moved along the coast, had to be redirected to safer interior routes. Normally, most oil on the Barge Canal moved westward. During the war, though, more came from the Great Lakes east to the Atlantic to meet military and civilian demands. There was a peak of 168,000 barrels a day on the canal system during the heavier periods of submarine warfare.[24]

By 1950, a report of the President's Water Resources Policy Commission had concluded that oil barges were a better use of resources than were railroad cars, especially when resources were limited, as during wartime. The report noted that a skilled workforce and 24 tons of steel were required for a 240-barrel railroad gasoline tank car, while a simple barge easily could be built using 250 tons of steel and carry 10,000 barrels of oil. Generally, supplies had been shipped by railroad during the war, and the commission concluded that decision makers failed to see "the potentialities of barge transportation [and] prevented the waterways from fully achieving their usefulness in the war job. This is a lesson that the Nation cannot afford to ignore as it prepares for future emergencies."[25] The government was so thankful for what the canal did move during the war that the *Rome Sears*, a 14,000-barrel oil tank barge, was awarded the U. S. Navy's Certificate of Achievement for its outstanding transportation record during the war.[26]

Although the St. Lawrence Seaway was the major factor in the decline of the grain traffic on the Barge, it was only one of the many factors that eventually caused a reduction of petroleum traffic. A newspaper report in 1961 noted that fuel shipments had declined since 1957. "Competition from the St. Lawrence Seaway for petroleum and other shipments and a general economic decline that hit all waterways were among the factors in the 1960 drop-off, the state Public Works Department said Friday. Heating oil shipments were down because of high inventories remaining for the mild winter of 1959–60. In addition, high water last spring shortened the canal season."[27]

Petroleum pipelines in New York State took a large part of the canal's traffic (oil is one of the few products that can be moved great distances by pipeline). By 1951 there were underground pipelines pumping petroleum from refineries in Pennsylvania to Rochester, Syracuse, and Buffalo, and from Buffalo to Rochester and Syracuse. The rates for shipping oil by pipelines were at the time about equivalent to canal transport, but what really gave the pipelines an advantage was the common carrier, or public line, put in place by the Buckeye Pipe Line Company from two seaboard ports in New Jersey and Pennsylvania. This system had a much greater capacity than the other pipelines and a terse statement in one of the reports on New York State waterways in 1951 summarizes this concern: "This line, when complete, will offer keen competition to barge operations in Western New York."[28]

The petroleum pipelines were successful because they were not affected by weather, as the canal was, and they easily operated year round. That advantage also meant that the oil companies did not have to store a complete winter's supply at each locality, an expensive burden. A 1958 Utica observer wrote that the customary "winter stoppage has forced oil marketers in this section to add substantial product storage facilities to carry them over such a slack period. In the light of a more certain supply of distillate fuel oils and gasoline through the use of the

Oil barges such as the *Cayuga Sun*, shown here in 1935, moved oil across New York State. The pilot house is in the center of the motorship and the living quarters are at the stern.
New York State Archives

pipeline, their requirements can be filled on a more concise and regular basis. Thus their storage facilities may be converted to heavy oil stockpiling, which it is believed will further dampen the outlook for barge deliveries through the canal system."[29]

Rochester provides another example. In 1950, 416,875 tons of oil moved into the city by canal; in 1953 the city was still receiving 278,989 tons. In 1954 a pipeline was extended to Rochester—only 33,159 tons of oil were shipped by canal to the city that year.[30]

A traveler on the Barge Canal today can see remnants of the petroleum heydays. Jutting out of the canal banks here and there are pipes once used to load nearby oil storage tanks. Some of these tanks are still alongside the canal; some are still used, filled now by railroad, truck, or pipeline.

Many products shipped on the Barge Canal saw years of high tonnage and then faded while another item became prominent. In 1959 a state canal official said in response to the St. Lawrence Seaway's taking of canal commerce, "You lose one thing and pick up another . . . The traffic pattern is changing."[31]

Ten products were shipped in amounts greater than 100,000 tons per year in the early decades of the canal but by 1951 were either gone from the canal or moved in much smaller quantities: flour, rye, barley, sugar, flaxseed, lumber, anthracite coal, iron ore, iron or steel products, and sand, stone, or gravel. Factors that caused the shipments of each of these to decline vary with the product. Sugar, for instance, peaked at over 400,000 tons in 1932 and 1933. Still over 100,000 tons were shipped annually until 1940, when it vanished from the canal during World War II because of rationing and short supplies. After the war, the canal did not recapture the sugar traffic. It had been moved on the railroad during the war, and having adjusted to these less-than-barge-load quantities, companies were reluctant to give up the more manageable and regular railroad shipments. (Trucking had also become a more viable competitor.) Also during the war, the importation of sugar was redirected to southern ports and then inland, instead of through New York, due to the danger of German submarines off the Atlantic Coast. After the war, sugar continued to be barged out of New Orleans through Mississippi and Illinois waterways to Toledo, Detroit, and Cleveland.[32] Additionally, domestic corn syrup replaced sugar in some processing.

In 1950, the year before traffic on the Barge Canal hit its all-time peak of just over 5.2 million tons, a private committee concerned with New York State waterways reported in its *Economic Survey of the Barge Canal* that 11 products made up

Above:
This 1922 view of the Buffalo Terminal shows sugar being unloaded from a canal barge to a lake steamer by crane. Sugar had a relatively brief life on the Barge Canal, with none being shipped after World War II.

New York State Archives

Left:
In 1922, views such as this one of sand being loaded from a barge onto a horse drawn wagon by crane at Syracuse were common. The freight house in the background still stands at the canal harbor in Syracuse.

New York State Archives

more than 94 percent of all canal traffic. Over 50,000 tons of each product were shipped that year. The largest volume by far was petroleum oil, accounting for more than 30 times the tonnage of wheat, the next largest product. Corn also moved on the canal that year, over 100,000 tons eastward to Albany (down from a peak of 704,365 tons in 1938).[33]

Molasses, used to make feed for cattle, was an important item shipped on the canal. Ocean tankers brought molasses from the Caribbean to storage tanks at Albany; from there, canal barges took it across the state to Buffalo, where it was processed and distributed to farmers and feed mills elsewhere. Because barges could carry large amounts, and because pumping and storage facilities in Albany and Buffalo were available, the canal was ideal for such a commodity.

Another bulk item shipped on the canal was fertilizer—about 82,000 tons were shipped in 1950. From Buffalo and New York City, fertilizer was shipped to Fulton, Newark, Baldwinsville, Niagara Falls, Brockport, Sylvan Beach, Pittsford, and Waterloo. In 1951 however, the rail rate for phosphate rock (a fertilizer ingredient) was reduced to the canal rate—the amount of fertilizer shipped on the canal fell to just 51,111 tons that year.[34]

The brick Buffalo warehouse was large enough to store many loads of goods from canal boats, waiting to be picked up or moved by rail, truck or ship. This view shows the interior in 1921.

New York State Archives

A LONG HAUL

Scrap iron moved in significant quantities in 1950, with most going to the Buffalo-Lackawanna steel mills from ports in New York, Connecticut, and Rhode Island. Indeed, tonnage that year approached the high-demand war years of the early 1940s.[35] Pig iron and billets (bars of iron ore that has been processed for later use in steel and other products) were shipped on the Barge Canal in 1950 from the Buffalo area to points around New York, New Jersey, Maryland, and Connecticut. Although there were some periods of very heavy shipments from 1927 to 1942, pig iron tonnage steadily declined afterwards to just 66,212 tons in 1949.[36] Iron ore mined in Port Henry also was shipped on the Champlain Canal and across the Erie Canal to Buffalo.

Two important chemicals shipped on the canal in 1950 were soda ash and liquid caustic soda. The ash was transported from Allied Chemical's Solvay plant, near Syracuse, to New Jersey; the liquid caustic soda (used in making lye and related products) went from a plant in Wyandotte, Michigan, to New York City. (Former canaler Bill Hills remembered making the mistake of walking through a yard at the Solvay plant that also held the white, powdery caustic soda he was about to haul. The next morning the work shoes he had worn the day before had

Loads of scrap iron moved on the Hudson River and Barge Canal west to the Lackawanna Steel Mills near Buffalo. These barges are tied on the dock wall in Troy in 1922.
New York State Archives

A fleet of wooden barges is moving nitrate of soda on the canal west of Lock 23 in 1921. Chemicals such as this were moved in large quantities on the canal from 1931 to 1941.

New York State Archives

dissolved—just the soles were left.) Although the decade from 1931 to 1941 saw heavy traffic of chemicals—over 200,000 tons per year—the shipments slacked off during the war. By 1950, the traffic amounted to just 42,866 tons.[37]

Another indication of how competitive rail rates affected canal shipments is demonstrated by sulfur (used to make sulfuric acid, essential for making fertilizers, drugs, detergents, dyes, lead acid, and other industrial products). The tonnage has varied widely since it first appeared in 1923. In 1938, a change in the rail rates helped cause a 60 percent decrease in the canal tonnage of sulfur. In 1949, only 6,327 tons went from Edgewater, New Jersey, to Buffalo; by 1950, 52,962 tons were shipped, still far short of its 1937 peak of 297,000 tons. Sulfur was also shipped on the Mississippi River, a route that was a major competitor for the canal's traffic in the product. In 1948 it was cheaper to send sulfur from Texas up the Mississippi to Chicago and then across the Great Lakes to Canada than it was to send it up the Atlantic seaboard to New York City and across the Barge Canal.[38]

The canal was heavily used by New York City metropolitan newspapers to move rolls of newsprint from paper mills in Canada. Newsprint barges were much smaller than the system's standard barge, carrying just 220 tons of the large rolls. (The paper came from Canadian mills on the St. Lawrence River; the barges were limited by the lock dimensions on the Chambly

A LONG HAUL

Canal, which bypasses rapids on the Richelieu River, a connection between Lake Champlain and the Saint Lawrence River.) In 1949, about half of the system's total newsprint traffic moved on the Champlain Canal, 40 percent on the Oswego Canal, and the remainder from points along the Erie. An essential ingredient of paper, pulpwood (most of which came down the Champlain Canal) had a small but steady tonnage record: There were 79,520 tons of pulpwood on the canal in 1950, up from only 12,000 tons the year before, but well below a 200,000-ton peak in 1947.[39]

While clearly the Barge Canal was ideal for these large-quantity, bulky freights, the waterway also was used for manufactured or specialty items. In 1921, a short-lived package freight service began between Rochester and New York City. At the time, an observer noted that "considerable quantities of photographic apparatus, optical goods, machinery and products of a like nature were moved via the waterway to New York for export. This was the first instance of the movement of export package freight in any volume via the canals."[40] These were interesting freight items, especially with the growing dominance of Rochester corporate giants such as Eastman Kodak and

Heavy loads were moved at the freight terminal in North Tonawanda with the help of a steel stiff-leg derrick. This imposing dock machinery was at other Barge Canal terminals as well. This 1922 view shows part of the bascule lift bridge in the background and the freight house behind the derrick.

New York State Archives

Bausch and Lomb. Another significant item was the copper that was shipped from Brazil and Washington state onto the Barge Canal for use at the wire company in Rome.[41]

One way to appreciate the diversity of the canal's traffic can be found in the experiences of just one tugboat. In 1939, Arthur "Blondie" Connor was a captain on the *Empire*, a tug that hauled barges with various loads. Connor's family has preserved a meticulous log that tracks his hectic boating life that year and lends insight into the nature of canal work in the 1930s.[42]

For example, on August 6 Connor spent almost two hours after midnight in Troy gathering a tow of eight barges to move down the Hudson River to different docks in New York harbor. He spent the next few days around New York City, hiring himself and the tug out to move boats from dock to dock while waiting for a tow of barges to take back up to the canal. With a new tow of six barges he went back up the Hudson, delivering two barges at the dock in Troy and taking the remaining four on to Waterford.

The tug made two separate trips through the five locks of the Waterford flight to get the four barges through, working from 11 PM to 4 AM. Connor was taking the barges light to Solvay to pick up a load, a two-and-a-half-day trip. The tug did not stop, day or night, except at the locks. He left the barges at a dock in Solvay to be loaded (probably with nitrate of soda), then returned about a half day later to pick them up. He spent the loading time getting small jobs moving barges between Syracuse and Solvay. It was now August 16.

Connor brought the tow of four loaded barges east to Erie Lock 13, where he swapped with another tug for a light tow that had been headed west. He then returned to Solvay, now with a new string of empty barges. While these barges were taking on their loads at Solvay, he was again keeping busy with small towing jobs in the area, this time to Oswego.

He kept up this kind of towing schedule until his first break on September 13, when he took two days off. He had made few stops during this five weeks of towing. His log notes indicate that they were purely business related—to refill water barrels, take on fuel (usually about 2,000 gallons at a time), wait for fog, make repairs, wait for barge crews to stock up on grub and get their pay checks, wait for wind to subside, clear up an accident (the cook fell over the oil barrel), and wait for additional crews on the barges. He was often delayed at the locks while waiting for other boats ahead of him to pass (once for six-and-a-half hours at Lock 17). He had to wait when the barges needed repairs along the way, too, or when they needed to fill up on water. He was sometimes left waiting for orders on where to pick up his next tow of barges.

Another perspective on the canal's traffic is shown by a sampling of miscellaneous freight on the canal reported in 1934 and 1935 by the superintendent of public works. The report listed such things as chalk, graphite, almonds, coffee, flowers, nutmeg, peanuts, bird seed, cold cream, toys, wax, linoleum, and tea.[43]

Local newspapers carried accounts of other special products being carried on the canal, as well:

> The first shipment of knit goods from the Mohawk Valley by way of the barge canal was made a few days ago by William Bros. Manufacturing Co. of this city [Rome]. It was a government order of underwear for US soldiers now in France. [1918][44]

> The motorship Buckeye State is due to pass Rome tomorrow loaded with 40 tons of 3.2 legal beer. This is the first shipment of the legal beverage to be transported by canal. [1933][45]

> Nearly $100,000 worth of eels passed through Rome yesterday via the Barge Canal, enroute to New York, for the Thanksgiving

The *Buckeye State*, built in 1930, was a motorship that once shipped 40 tons of beer among other diverse cargoes. The boat is approaching Erie Barge Lock 3 in Waterford, passing a group of state boats, about 1931.

New York State Archives

trade. The fish, from Quebec, were aboard two specially designed steel boats containing 35 tons apiece. Eels sell for 69-70 cents a pound wholesale. [1938][46]

There were shipped, via canal, over 60,000 pieces of snow removal equipment weighing about 150 tons, to New York. The shipment was consigned to several hardware jobbers in New York City for redistribution throughout the Metropolitan district. [1934][47]

The world's largest ship model, the Queen Mary, continued on its journey to the New York World's Fair this morning after an overnight stop here. The scale model is 22 feet long and 31 inches wide and has a maximum speed of 15 miles an hour. The vessel carries a two-man crew, but has room for three. It will go on exhibit at the New York Fair. [1939][48]

Two torpedo boats, marked PT3 and 4, believed the first of some 60 of their type, passed Rome yesterday on the Barge Canal. They are 56 feet long and have a 14 foot beam. [1940][49]

One of the strangest tows ever to go through the Barge Canal has arrived in Utica. The first of two purifier tanks to be towed from the Syracuse gas plant of the Central New York Power Corporation to the company's Utica gas plant. The huge, tar-coated cylinder, 30 feet in diameter, 16 feet high and weighing nearly 30 tons, was lashed to the stern of the tug, Seneca. [1947][50]

Eels also made the trip from Quebec through the Champlain Canal in specially designed barges with open bottoms:

> The eels are caught in specially constructed nets at the upper end of the St. Lawrence River. They are bought alive from the fishermen and placed aboard specially constructed barges for transportation. [In the barges], there is a space of about one inch between each plank to permit the water to pass through. Between the bulkheads, the barges are divided into compartments, into which the eels are placed for transportation . . . The eels average around four pounds each. Fifty to eighty tons of eels are brought down annually in this manner. [1934][51]

By 1921, "the sending of automobiles by canal had become so common as to have lost its novelty."[52] In 1926, the state's superintendent of public works reported that the loss of some of the grain trade on the Oswego Canal in 1925 was made up for by the increase shipping of specialty manufactured items of higher value. He concluded, "This is mostly due to the transportation of automobiles and parts from Great Lakes ports

to New York via the canal port of Oswego and the canal route
east thereof."[53]

Henry Ford vacationed on the Barge Canal in 1922, stimu-
lating his interest in using the canal to move his car parts. In
1931 he launched two motorships designed for travel on the
Great Lakes, the Barge Canal, and the Atlantic. The Ford Motor
Company used the canal to ship car parts between East Coast
ports and Michigan. Axles, springs, radiators, and other finished
auto parts were carried by barge to Ford's River Rouge plant in
Dearborn, Michigan, from four manufacturing plants in the
East, all located along navigable waterways—Chester,
Pennsylvania; Edgewater, New Jersey; Green Island, New York
(along the Hudson River); and Norfolk, Virginia. Similarly,
boxed export parts traveled from the River Rouge plant to
eastern ports for shipment overseas. Not surprisingly, the four
motorships in this service were named the *Chester*, the
Edgewater, the *Green Island*, and the *Norfolk*.

The *Chester* and *Edgewater* were put into service in 1931. They
were 300 feet long with a capacity of 2,800 tons and carried a
crew of 22. They had such modifications for canal travel as
retractable pilot houses and folding radio masts. In 1937, the

Automobiles were shipped on the canal
in significant quantities in the early
1920s. This view shows Maxwell autos at
Erie Barge Lock 11 in a tow with steel
rails in 1922, heading east.

New York State Archives

Green Island and *Norfolk* were built. With slightly larger capacities of 3,000 tons, they were noted at the time as being the world's largest ships with welded-steel hulls, a novel process at the time.[54]

The Ford motorships were in use on the canal until the early years of World War II. The federal government commandeered the vessels for the war effort, using them to move sugar up the coast from Cuba and to supply Great Britain via the North Atlantic. Ford protested that his boats were not designed for such use, to no avail. "All of the Ford canal carriers had long, low silhouettes, which led to at least one of them being mistaken for a submarine during World War II."[55] The *Green Island* was sunk by a German submarine; the other three were sold after the war's conclusion.

One of the last major commodities to be shipped on the Barge Canal was bulk cement. The self-unloading *Day Peckinpaugh* began carrying it in 1961 from Picton, Ontario, to Oswego and through the canal to Rome. As a general hauler, the vessel already had a long career on the canal, beginning in 1921 as the *I.L.I. 101* (later know as the *Richard J. Barnes*). It was proclaimed on its maiden voyage to be the first of the motorships specifically

Opposite:
Top: One of the boats owned by the Ford Company to ship auto parts was the *Chester*, here coming out of Lock 5 in Waterford about 1939. The low profile of the four barges the company built for the canal caused at least one to be mistaken as a submarine during war service and torpedoed during World War II.

New York State Museum (Michon Collection)

Bottom: The bow of the *Interwaterways Line Incorporated 101*, locked down at Erie Barge Lock 7 in this 1921 view, looks very similar to its present appearance as the *Day Peckinpaugh*, a later version of the craft taken off the canal in 1994. Notice the hatches on top of the deck where bulk material was loaded into the boat's cargo hold for transport.

Canal Society of New York State (Gayer Collection)

Below:
These lumber barges were unloaded by hand at the Mechanicville Terminal on the Champlain Canal in 1923.

New York State Archives

designed for the larger dimensions of the state's new canal system. Shipping this new commodity was seen at the time as "the forerunner of a whole new dynamic trend . . . or . . . the dying gasp of a once proud and economically important waterway."[56]

In retrospect, the analogy to the dying gasp is probably more accurate. The *Day Peckinpaugh* was the last great motorship to see service on the New York State Barge Canal System. This 251-foot-long motorship was a grand presence on the canal, making 30 to 40 round trips every season from Oswego to Rome. It carried 1,500 tons of dry cement that were transferred to one of six storage silos in Rome. The cement was bagged at the Rome facility, then trucked to markets in eastern New York and western New England. In 1961 the Mohawk Valley Cement Company, which received the barge shipments, estimated its cargo to be 100,000 tons per year.[57] It would have taken 82 tractor trailers to replace the amount held in the *Peckinpaugh* in one trip. "Water is just about the best way to deliver cement. The obvious thing was to locate on the canal where we could take advantage of low-cost waterborne bulk deliveries," said W. H. Jagels, manager of the Mohawk Valley Cement Company when the company began the operation.[58]

Although sights such as this 1935 view of this commercial barge, the *Bernie*, built in 1928, and its tug, *Protector*, built in 1899, entering Lock 14 in Canajoharie are gone, the lock structure, gates and machinery are still there to admire. Pleasure boats fill this lock today and picnickers and people fishing enjoy the park atmosphere at this lock lined with willow trees along the Mohawk River.

New York State Archives

A LONG HAUL

On the vessel's last trip on the canal in 1994, a crew member reflected on the Barge Canal's commercial traffic: "Even ten years ago there was a lot of commercial traffic. You might have one [barge] behind you and a couple up ahead . . . Everything that could float was on this canal. We pretty well have the canal to ourselves, now."[59]

By the 1960s, state budget cutters were beginning to feel burdened by the maintenance costs of the canal. "We were under pressure all the time to save money and cut back," said Joseph Stellato, former head of canal operations, during this first of several tough fiscal times.[60] A controversial suggestion had already been made to transfer ownership (and thus maintenance costs) of the Barge Canal to the federal government. (In fact, in 1959 New York State voters approved a constitutional amendment that would have allowed the federal government to take over the canal.)

The issue arose because the canal needed modernization, especially with the new competition of the St. Lawrence Seaway. The federal government, through the Army Corps of Engineers, had already been active in projects on the Ohio and Mississippi waterways that improved their commercial potential. An upstate newspaper editorial asked, "We support the Mississippi

The Barge Canal was created as an avenue of commerce. Businesses such as the People's Ice Company in Syracuse depended on the canal to ship their products, in this case ice being loaded at the Syracuse Terminal in 1921.
New York State Archives

waterways, do we not? . . .Then let Mississippians contribute to the New York canal."[61] It was hoped the canal would be enlarged if the federal government took it over, an improvement that would be welcomed by current users and that would broaden the possibilities of new users of the canal.

Those opposed to the transfer of the canal worried that the state would lose the canal for conservation and flood control, as a water supply for upstate farms, for power generation, and for recreational use.[62] People even worried that the federal government would deepen the canal and, in doing so, drain lakes in the Adirondacks and central New York.[63] "A lot of people shared the opinion that they wouldn't build it in the first place, why give it to them now?" Stellato stated, reflecting on the federal government's refusal to help build the Erie in the early nineteenth century.[64]

Despite these concerns, the people of the state voted to give the canal to the federal government. Just as when the original Barge Canal Law was passed, this transfer proposition was carried with New York City votes. After the vote, the completion of the transfer required the state legislature's approval. For a few years bills were introduced in the legislature but all failed—the state's political leaders never agreed to turn over the Barge Canal to the federal government.

At the same time this debate was occurring, the federal government was trying to decide if it even wanted the canal. The Army Corps of Engineers made several studies of the costs and benefits of improving, or simply rehabilitating, the canal (an improved and enlarged canal probably would have flooded out a few villages, such as Tribes Hill and Baldwinsville). Engineering studies included plans to enlarge the locks up to 600 feet long by 100 feet wide, to increase the clearance under bridges by raising them, and to straighten curves while widening the channel. Governor Rockefeller recommended that the canal be rehabilitated instead of enlarged.[65] The Corps of Engineers concluded that the canal would not be able to carry boats large enough to justify the expense of the rehabilitation, and eventually the plan to transfer the Barge Canal to the federal government was abandoned.

Today, the largest boats seen on the waterway are yachts and tour boats. It is almost completely a canal for tourists, either in their own boats or on a cruise ship. There were about 12,000 pleasure-boat permits issued in 1995, more than double the 1958 figure. (In turn, the 1958 figure was double the number of just four years earlier.)[66] While commercial traffic declined through these years, pleasure-boat traffic began to climb dramatically, a trend that is still continuing. By 1966, officials clearly saw the possibility of the canal as a recreation site. One stated that "the full potential of the waterway for fishing, swimming, boating, picnicking has not been tapped."[67]

Although there always have been pleasure boats using the canal (917 of them as early as 1935), recreational use of the canal today has taken the place of commercial shipping in the state's long-term goals for the waterway. In 1992, operation of the New York State Barge Canal System was transferred from the New York State Department of Transportation to the New York State Thruway Authority as part of the Thruway 2000 plan. As part of the transfer, the legislature established the Canal Corporation within the Thruway Authority to run the canal, focusing on recreation and shore-side economic development. The Canal Corporation is now courting the boaters.

Another product of the transfer was the 1995 Canal Recreationway Plan. Three goals inspired the plan—to preserve the best of the past, to enhance recreational opportunities, and to foster economic development along the canal corridor. The canal needed to become a "linear park" that showcased boating

Pleasure boats share the pier with commercial barges and tugs on the canal in Brewerton around 1950. Pleasure boats eventually outnumbered commercial vessels on the waterway so that now pleasure boats are the primary craft that use the canal.

Canal Society of New York State

The Utica Harbor freight terminal, newly built in this 1922 view, is still there today, being used by the state's canal maintenance forces.

New York State Archives

opportunities and the historic and aesthetic qualities of the waterway. Full implementation of the plan had a price tag of $146 million, but the source of that funding was debated. In 1996 the federal Department of Housing and Urban Development launched a $120-million program to implement much of what was in the state's Recreationway Plan.

Not only was the Recreationway Plan promoting use of the canal by boaters, it was also encouraging land-side use of the waterway. The plan strongly urged that the bike and hiking trails alongside the canal (which already existed) be connected so there would be a complete state-wide network. The plan encouraged the development of services and facilities in areas that were already developed so as not to spoil the canal's more scenic areas. "The pristine parts of the canal will be preserved," says John Jermano, member of the Recreationway Commission and director of operations for the canal from 1985 to 1995. He concludes that "we're in the rebirth of the canal."[68]

The Recreationway Plan called for canal landings to ensure that needed services were available at regular intervals. The seven largest of these landings, called harbor centers, were designated at the Tonawandas, Rochester, Seneca Falls, Oswego, Little Falls, Waterford, and Whitehall. (Another canal harbor at Syracuse had been designated earlier by the Thruway 2000 legislation.) "Harbor centers will increase the awareness and usability of the canal," says Jermano. "The canals need to stimulate recreational use and economic development. Both will be found at the harbor centers."[69]

Indeed, communities along its banks are beginning to see the value of the canal to their economic and cultural well being. It is no longer seen as a backyard nuisance. In Fairport, for example, the canal-side environment has been improved and now draws neighbors, visitors, and business. In nearby Pittsford, a group of

Pleasure boats leave Lock 11 on the
Champlain Canal in August 1962.
New York State Archives

new shops inhabit old warehouses along the canal's banks.
Communities sponsor Canal Days to celebrate the waterway and
to show that their heritage and identity are linked to the canal.
Picnic areas, hiking trails, boating facilities, and parking areas are
bringing people to the water's edge, where they can see
themselves and their communities' futures reflected in the
potential of the waterway.

Today's canalers, on the water and on the shore, also have the
privilege of seeing remnants of the state's earlier canals along the
newer waterway. The stonework from the nineteenth-century
aqueducts, locks, and culverts lies within sight of the Barge
Canal, a visual link to the days of mules and drivers that ties us to
New York State's two centuries of canal heritage.

Today's canal is filled with such connections, from past to
present to future, from the Hudson River to Lake Erie, from
village to village, and from generation to generation. The canal
has carried it all. It truly has been a long haul.

Notes

INTRODUCTION

1. *Barge Canal Bulletin* (June 1909), 210.
2. Noble E. Whitford, *History of the Barge Canal of New York State* (Albany: J. B. Lyon Company, Printers, 1922), 50.
3. Ibid., 514.
4. Ibid., 9.

CHAPTER 1

1. Whitford, *History of the Barge Canal*, 50.
2. Richard Garrity, *Canal Boatman: My Life on Upstate Waterways* (Syracuse: Syracuse University Press, 1977), 115.
3. Whitford, 355.
4. "Concrete Barge Sinks at Dock," *Engineering News-Record* (7 August 1919), 292.
5. *Barge Canal Bulletin* (March 1918), 74.
6. Joseph H. Salmon, *Economic Survey of the New York State Barge Canal* (Economic Survey Committee for New York State Waterways, 1951), 23.
7. Whitford, 391.
8. Salmon, 20.
9. Dennis Fishette, interview by author, 6 June 1995, Barge Canal Inspection Tour.
10. John Jermano, interview by author, 6 June 1995, Barge Canal Inspection Tour.
12. The distance includes Seneca and Cayuga Lakes.
12. Larry O'Connor, interview by author, 11 October 1995, Barge Canal Inspection Tour.
13. John Jermano, interview by author, 9 June 1994, Barge Canal Inspection Tour.
14. Ibid.
15. Bill Clifford, interview by author, 9 June 1994, Barge Canal Inspection Tour.
16. "The Oswego Canal Field Trip Guide, 14 October 1989" (Syracuse: Canal Society of New York State, 1989), 24.
17. William N. Embree, "Water-Level Control in the New York State Canal System Within the Oswego River Basin," (Albany: U. S. Department of the Interior, 1993), 6.
18. Ibid., 8.

CHAPTER 2

1. Editorial, *Fairport Herald*, 22 July 1903.
2. *Barge Canal Bulletin* (June 1909), 210.
3. Whitford, *History of the Barge Canal*, 16.
4. *Barge Canal Bulletin* (June 1909), 221.
5. Whitford, 35.
6. Ibid., 47.
7. Ibid., 51.
8. Edward A. Bond, *Report on the Barge Canal from the Hudson River to the Great Lakes* (Albany: James B. Lyon, State Printer, 1901), 11.
9. Ibid., 4.
10. Ibid., 6.
11. Whitford, 75–76.
12. Ibid., 77.
13. Ibid., 82.
14. "More Costly Than All Our Schools," *Fairport Herald*, 7 October 1903.
15. Editorial, *Fairport Herald*, 22 April 1903.
16. Editorial, *Fairport Herald*, 30 September 1903.
17. Editorial, *Fairport Herald*, 22 July 1903.
18. "Route Of The New Barge Canal Through Fairport," *Fairport Herald*, 11 November 1903.
19. "The Black River Canal," *Rome Daily Sentinel*, 12 January 1903.
20. "Business On The Canals," *Rome Daily Sentinel*, 3 August 1903.
21. "The Barge Canal in Rome," *Rome Daily Sentinel*, 24 October 1903.
22. Ibid.
23. Editorial, *Rome Daily Sentinel*, 24 January 1903.
24. "The New Canal," *Rome Daily Sentinel*, 3 July 1903.
25. Editorial, *Rome Daily Sentinel*, 24 January 1903.
26. "The New Canal," *Rome Daily Sentinel*, 3 July 1903.
27. Whitford, 127.
28. Editorial, *Rome Daily Sentinel*, 21 July 1903.
29. Whitford, 129.
30. Ibid., 131.
31. Ibid., 132–133.
32. M. M. Wilner, "The New York State Press in the Campaign for Enlargement of the Canals," in *Buffalo Historical Society Publications* 13 (1909), 193.
33. "Barge Canal Proposition is Carried," *Fairport Herald*, 4 November 1903.
34. "The Sovereign City," *Rome Daily Sentinel*, 7 November 1903.

CHAPTER 3

1. Roy G. Finch, *The Story of the New York State Canals* (Albany: J. B. Lyon Co., 1925), 17.
2. Whitford, *History of the Barge Canal*, 211.

3. "Housing Conditions and Wages on the New York State Barge Canal and on the Ashokan Dam, Board of Water Supply, New York City," *Engineering News-Record*, 5 August 1909, 154.

4. "Canal Claims Reach $500,000," undated article in Earl Scothon scrapbook (Albany: Collection of New York State Museum).

5. Ibid.

6. Ibid.

7. Bill Orzell did much of the pioneering research on this topic. See *Bottoming Out*, Number 33 (1996): 10–30.

8. Whitford, 446.

9. *Annual Report of the Superintendent of Public Works*, 1921, 158.

10. Editorial, *Rome Daily Sentinel*, 21 February 1930.

11. *Barge Canal Bulletin* (April 1908), 70.

12. Ibid., 72.

13. Ibid.

14. Whitford, 232.

15. *Barge Canal Bulletin* (January 1909), 26.

16. *Barge Canal Bulletin* (June 1908), 146.

17. *Barge Canal Bulletin* (November 1910), 444.

18. *Barge Canal Bulletin* (March 1914), 109.

19. "Field Trip Guide October 6–8 1995: The Champlain Canal—Northumberland to Whitehall" (Syracuse: Canal Society of New York State), 47.

20. *Barge Canal Bulletin* (June 1910), 207.

21. *Barge Canal Bulletin* (May 1910), 168.

22. Whitford, 494.

23. *Barge Canal Bulletin* (January 1914), 33.

24. Whitford, 214.

25. Ibid., 215.

26. Ibid., 216.

27. Ibid., 220.

28. "The Cayuga & Seneca Canal Field Trip" (Syracuse: Canal Society of New York State, 1989), 5.

29. "Field Trip Guide May 20, 1995: The Erie Canal—Monroe and Orleans Counties" (Syracuse: Canal Society Of New York State, 1995), 44.

30. Garrity, *Canal Boatman*, 120.

31. *Annual Report of the Superintendent of Public Works*, 1925, 173.

32. Ibid., 16.

33. Ibid., 196.

34. Whitford, 199–200.

35. Ibid., 199.

36. Ibid., 200.

37. Ibid., 206.

38. "The Oswego Canal Field Trip Guide, 14 October 1989," (Syracuse: Canal Society of New York State, 1989), 27.

39. Ibid.

40. H. Lee White Maritime Museum in Oswego has a display explaining the Oswego Grain Elevator.

41. *Annual Report of the Superintendent of Public Works*, 1933, 11.
42. Salmon, *Economic Survey of the New York State Barge Canal*, 23.
43. *Barge Canal Bulletin* (June 1918), 163.
44. *Rochester Democrat & Chronicle*, 19 May 1918.
45. *Knickerbocker Press*, 4 July 1918.

CHAPTER 4

1. Whitford, *History of the Barge Canal*, 466.
2. *Barge Canal Bulletin* (February 1910), 46.
3. Whitford, 485.
4. Ibid., 481.
5. Ibid.
6. *Barge Canal Bulletin* (April 1917), 100.
7. "Field Trip Guide May 20, 1995: The Erie Canal—Monroe and Orleans Counties," 60.
8. Whitford, 337.
9. "Field Trip Guide May 20 1995: The Erie Canal—Monroe and Orleans Counties," 44–45.
10. *Barge Canal Bulletin* (July 1910), 315.
11. *Barge Canal Bulletin* (August 1910), 351.
12. Ibid., 347.
13. Whitford, 492.
14. Ibid.
15. Bill Hills, interview by author, 9 June 1995, Barge Canal Inspection Tour.
16. *Barge Canal Bulletin* (October 1909), 373.
17. Whitford, 472.
18. Ibid., 472–473.
19. Ibid.
20. Ibid., 471.
21. Ibid., 478.
22. Ibid.

CHAPTER 5

1. *Barge Canal Bulletin* (June 1910), 214.
2. Bill Pittsley, interview by author, 18 January 1996, Brewerton (Lock 23).
3. "Canallers [sic] Have Unique Mail System on Inland Waterways," article, 20 August 1961, in Earl Scothon scrapbook.
4. Pittsley, interview.
5. "New York State Canal System Monthly Traffic Report 1995 Navigation Season" (Albany: New York State Thruway Authority, 1995).
6. "Daily Report Passages—Floats—Lockages Lock 23," 12 September 1965 (Albany: New York State Department of Transportation, 1965).

7. Pittsley, interview.

8. Calvin Pendergrass, interview by Craig Williams, 6 November 1977, Little Falls.

9. Dennis Fishette, interview by author, 6 June 1995, Canal Inspection Tour.

10. Ibid.

11. Crew of *Peckinpaugh*, video interview by Craig Williams, September 1994, Oneida Lake (Albany: Collection of New York State Museum).

12. "Canallers *[sic]* Have Unique Mail System on Inland Waterways," op. cit.

13. Ibid.

14. Fishette, interview.

15. "Quick Thinking, Bravery Prevent Canal Tragedy," D.C.T. Newsletter, April 1968, in Earl Scothon scrapbook.

16. Lock Operator's Log Book, 1956, Champlain Barge Canal Lock 5.

17. Whitford, 314.

18. Pendergrass, interview.

19. Article, 22 July 1940, in Earl Scothon scrapbook.

20. Article, 16 March 1941, in Earl Scothon scrapbook.

21. *Barge Canal Bulletin* (October 1910), 430.

22. Whitford, 314.

23. *Barge Canal Bulletin* (April 1908), 71.

24. "Our Canal Bridge, One of a Kind," *Fairport Herald*, 30 August 1978.

25. Ibid.

CHAPTER 6

1. "The Empire State's Navy," pamphlet (New York State Department of Transportation Waterways Maintenance Division, 1988).

2. "Floating Plant Vessels Assigned By Region and Section," (Albany: New York State Thruway Authority, 1995).

3. Frederick S. Greene and Thomas F. Farrell, *The New York State Canal System* (Albany: State Public Works Building, n.d.), 13.

4. Dan Geist, interview by author, 27 September 1996, Albany.

5. Fishette, interview.

6. Dennis Granley, interview by author, 6 December 1996, Three Rivers Point.

7. Desmond Dixie, interview by author, 6 December 1996, Three Rivers Point.

8. Ralph Folger, interview by author, 28 September 1996, Rensselaer.

9. Article, 30 March 1935, in Earl Scothon scrapbook.

10. Article, 26 March 1945, in Earl Scothon scrapbook.

11. Geist, interview.

12. Granley, interview.

13. Pendergrass, interview.

14. Chuck Dwyer, interview by Craig Williams, March 1994, Utica.

15. Ibid.

16. "Crew of Tug Praised for Heroic Work," article, 27 October 1926, in Earl Scothon scrapbook.

17. Ibid.

18. Ibid.

19. "Fleet Swept by Fifty-Mile Wind 12 Hours," undated article, in Earl Scothon scrapbook.

20. "Dredge Cutting Channel To Reach Stranded Vessel," undated article, in Earl Scothon scrapbook.

21. Dwyer, interview.

22. "Lake Canal's 'Weak Link,'" undated article, in Earl Scothon scrapbook.

23. "Canal Fleets Break Way Through Ice, Reach Rome," *Rome Daily Sentinel*, 4 December 1936.

24. Article, 20 December 1936, in Earl Scothon scrapbook.

25. "Canal Fleets Break Way Through Ice, Reach Rome," *Rome Daily Sentinel*, 4 December 1936.

26. Tom Prindle, "The Tugboat Urger: Ancient Mariner of the Barge Canal," *Sea History*, Summer 1991, 7–8.

27. Card File, New York State Department of Transportation.

28. "Housewife's 'Fun' Bid Buys State Yacht for $12,590," article, 21 November 1963, in Earl Scothon scrapbook.

29. Bill Orzell, "Headwaters of the New Deal," in *Bottoming Out* Number 29 (1994): 12.

30. Ibid., 7.

CHAPTER 7

1. Evamay Wilkins, interview by Craig Williams, 25 May 1993, Waterford.

2. Ibid.

3. "Down to the Sea in Barges, Back to the West Again," article, 25 August 1935, in Earl Scothon scrapbook.

4. Ibid.

5. Evamay Wilkins, interview by Craig Williams, 25 May 1993.

6. Evamay Wilkins, interview by Craig Williams, 25 June 1993.

7. Ibid.

8. Evamay Wilkins, interview by Craig Williams, 20 May 1993.

9. Ibid.

10. Wilkins, interview by Craig Williams, 25 June 1993.

11. Vessel Registration Forms, Series 17694 (Albany: New York State Archives).

12. Wilkins, interview by Craig Williams, 20 May 1993.

13. Wilkins, interview by Craig Williams, 27 July 1993.

14. Wilkins, interview by Craig Williams, 20 May 1993.

15. Joseph Mosso, interview by author, 28 September 1996, Rensselaer.

16. Wilkins, interview by Craig Williams, 20 May 1993.

17. Ibid.

18. Austin Huftill, interview by Craig Williams, 8 February 1994.

19. Ibid.

20. Ibid.

21. Wilkins, interview by Craig Williams, 25 June 1993.

22. Wilkins, interview by Craig Williams, 20 May 1993.

23. Wilkins, interview, by Craig Williams, 25 May 1993.

24. Evamay Wilkins, interview by author, 28 September 1996, Rensselaer.

25. Mosso, interview.

26. Ibid.

27. *Annual Report of the Superintendent of Public Works*, 1936, 7.

28. "Canal Still Useful Link in State's Economy," *Rome Daily Sentinel*, 1 December 1958.

29. Ibid.

30. "Trip on A Tugboat: A Working View Of 150-Year-Old Canal," *Buffalo Evening News*, 17 June 1967.

31. Article, 15 September 1966, in Earl Scothon scrapbook.

32. Ibid.

33. Wilkins, interview by Craig Williams, 25 June 1993, 44.

34. Article, 15 September 1966, in Earl Scothon scrapbook.

35. "Trip On A Tugboat: A Working View Of 150-Year-Old Canal," op. cit.

36. Article, 15 September 1966, in Earl Scothon scrapbook.

37. Fred Godfrey, *Sailors, Waterways and Tugboats I Have Known* (Monroe, NY: Library Research Associates, 1993), 15.

38. "She Tugs Through Life" article, February 1965, in Earl Scothon scrapbook.

39. Ibid.

40. Nelson Costello, interview by Craig Williams, 23 January 1997, Ticonderoga.

41. Folger, interview.

42. Mosso, interview.

43. Wilkins, interview by Craig Williams, 25 June 1993.

44. Charles T. O'Malley, *Low Bridges and High Water on the New York State Barge Canal* (Ellenton, FL: Diamond Mohawk Publishing, 1991), 249.

45. Ibid., 123.

46. "Assignment: The Bible on the Barge Canal," *Bible Society Record* (November 1958), in Earl Scothon scrapbook.

47. O'Malley, 136.

48. "Assignment: The Bible on the Barge Canal," op cit.

49. Ibid.

50. O'Malley, 138.

51. Dan Wiles, telephone interview by author, 31 March 1997.

52. Ibid.

53. Ibid.

54. Bill and Sue Orzell, interview by author, 8 August 1996, DeRuyter.

55. Ibid.

56. Ibid.

57. Ibid.

58. Ibid.

59. Ibid.

60. "385 Boats Winter-Locked in Canals Worst Tie-Up," *Rome Daily Sentinel*, 2 December 1936.

61. "Hopes Still Held For 5 Lake Ships," *Syracuse Journal*, 8 December 1936.

62. "Boats Battle Ice: Half Mile of Open Water," *Rome Daily Sentinel*, 3 December 1936.

63. "Barge Canal Freeze Traps 400 Craft," *Syracuse Herald*, 2 December 1936.
64. Ibid.
65. *Annual Report of the Superintendent of Public Works*, 1936, 7.

CHAPTER 8

1. "The Inception of the Barge Canal Project," in Buffalo Historical Society Publications 13 (1909), 119.
2. Whitford, *History of the Barge Canal*, 384.
3. "Tonnage on New York State Canals, 1900–[1979]." Unpublished report (Albany: New York State Department of Transportation, 1968).
4. *Annual Report of the Superintendent of Public Works*, 1924, 30.
5. *Annual Report of the Superintendent of Public Works*, 1936, 17.
6. "Oil Shipments on the New York State Canals." (New York State Radio Bureau), 17 October 1948.
7. Whitford, 19, 20.
8. Salmon, *Economic Survey of the New York State Barge Canal*, 23.
9. Article, 6 May 1921, in Earl Scothon scrapbook.
10. Salmon, 23.
11. "Barge Canal Is Losing Out To Both Seaway, Railroads," article, 7 August 1959, in Earl Scothon scrapbook.
12. *Annual Report of the Superintendent of Public Works*, 1933, 11.
13. Salmon, 24.
14. Ibid., 82–84.
15. Ibid., 20.
16. "Oil Shipments on the New York State Canals," op. cit.
17. Salmon, 21.
18. Ibid., 22.
19. Mosso, interview.
20. Whitford, 389.
21. "Canal's Largest Barges Being Outfitted," undated article, in Earl Scothon scrapbook.
22. Ibid.
23. Ibid.
24. Salmon, 56.
25. Ibid., 57.
26. Article, 8 January 1946, in Earl Scothon scrapbook.
27. "Barge Canal Shipments Show Decline," article, 11 February 1961, in Earl Scothon scrapbook.
28. Salmon, 64.
29. "New Oil Feeder Pipeline to Utica Expected to Hit Canal Service," article, October 1958, in Earl Scothon scrapbook.
30. "State of New York Report of the Joint Legislative Committee on The Barge Canal" (1961), 33.
31. "Barge Canal Is Losing Out To Both Seaway, Railroads," article, 7 August 1959, in Earl Scothon scrapbook.
32. Salmon, 19.

33. Ibid., 27.

34. Ibid., 30.

35. Ibid.

36. Ibid., 33.

37. Ibid., 31.

38. Ibid., 32.

39. Ibid., 37.

40. *Annual Report of the Superintendent of Public Works*, 1921, 10–11.

41. Article, 15 May 1922, in Earl Scothon scrapbook.

42. M. E. Connor, Log Book for Tug Empire 1939–1940 (Albany: Collection of New York State Museum).

43. *Annual Report of the Superintendent of Public Works*, 1934, 22; and *Annual Report of the Superintendent of Public Works*, 1935, 32.

44. Article, 27 May 1918, in Earl Scothon scrapbook.

45. Article, 11 July 1933, in Earl Scothon scrapbook.

46. Article, 18 November 1938, in Earl Scothon scrapbook.

47. *Annual Report of the Superintendent of Public Works*, 1934, 22–23.

48. Article, 25 June 1939, in Earl Scothon scrapbook.

49. Article, 20 June 1940, in Earl Scothon scrapbook.

50. Article, 28 October 1947, in Earl Scothon scrapbook.

51. *Annual Report of the Superintendent of Public Works*, 1934, 22–23.

52. Whitford, 391.

53. *Annual Report of The Superintendent of Public Works*, 1926, 27.

54. Clare J. Snider and Michael W. R. Davis, *The Ford Fleet (1923–1989)* (Cleveland, OH: Freshwater Press, 1994), 34–35.

55. Ibid.

56. "Canal Plays Key Role In New Cement Distribution Set-Up," in *New York Waterways* (March-April 1962), 4–6.

57. "First Bulk Shipment of Cement Arrives," article, 8 November 1961, in Earl Scothon scrapbook.

58. "Canal Plays Key Role In New Cement Distribution Set-up," op. cit., 4–6.

59. Crew of *Peckinpaugh*, video interview by Craig Williams, September 1994, Oneida Lake.

60. Joe Stellato, interview by Craig Williams, 16 January 1997, Loudonville.

61. "Barge Canal Giveaway or Tax Saver?" *Syracuse Herald*, 12 July 1959.

62. Ibid.

63. "Stormy Weather Ahead For Canal Committee," article, 14 January 1962, in Earl Scothon scrapbook.

64. Stellato, interview.

65. Ibid.

66. "The Barge Canal and Charts," August 1959, in Earl Scothon scrapbook.

67. "Let's Make Canal More Usable," article, 12 April 1966, in Earl Scothon scrapbook.

68. Jermano, interview.

69. Ibid.

Bibliography

Annual Report of the Superintendent Of Public Works. Albany: J. B. Lyon Company, Printers. 1921,
 1923, 1924, 1925, 1927, 1933, 1934, 1936.

Barge Canal Bulletin. Monthly. Department of the State Engineer and Surveyor of the State of
 New York. 1908–1919.

Bond, Edward Austin. *Report On The Barge Canal From The Hudson River to the Great Lakes.*
 Albany: James B. Lyon, State Printer, 1901.

Bottoming Out. Newsletter of the Canal Society of New York State. Number 29 (1994); Number 31
 and Number 32 (1995); Number 33 and Number 34 (1996).

Buffalo Evening News (New York). 17 June 1967.

"The Cayuga & Seneca Canal Field Trip." Syracuse: Canal Society of New York State, 1989.

Connor, M. E. Log Book For Tug *Empire*, 1939–1940. Albany: New York State Museum.

"Daily Report Passages—Floats—Lockages Lock 23." New York State Department of
 Transportation, 1965.

Edmonds, Walter Dumaux. *Rome Haul.* Syracuse: Syracuse University Press, 1929; rpt. 1987.

Embree, William N. "Water-Level Control in the New York State Canal System Within The
 Oswego River Basin—Description of Control Points and Guidelines to Their Operation."
 Albany: U. S. Department of the Interior, U. S. Geological Survey, 1993.

"The Empire State's Navy." New York State Department of Transportation Waterways Maintenance
 Division, 1988.

Engineering News-Record. 5 August 1909; 8 August 1918; 6 February 1919; 7 August 1919.

Fairport Herald (New York). 1903; 30 August 1978.

"Field Trip Guide May 20 1995: The Erie Canal—Monroe and Orleans Counties." Syracuse: Canal
 Society of New York State, 1995.

"Field Trip Guide October 6–8, 1995: The Champlain Canal—Northumberland to Whitehall."
 Syracuse: Canal Society of New York State, 1995.

"Field Trip Guide September 27–28, 1996: The Erie Canal, The Champlain Canal." Syracuse:
 Canal Society of New York State, 1996.

Finch, Roy G. *The Story of the New York Canals: Historical and Commercial Information.* Albany: J.
 B. Lyon Co., 1925.

"Floating Plant Vessels Assigned by Region and Section." New York State Thruway Authority, 1995.

Garrity, Richard. *Canal Boatman: My Life On Upstate Waterways.* Syracuse: Syracuse University
 Press, 1977.

Godfrey, Fred G. Sailors, *Waterways and Tugboats I Have Known: The New York State Barge Canal
 System.* Monroe, N.Y.: Library Research Associates Inc., 1993.

Gould, David R. "Dipper Dredge Number Three Research Report." Submitted to the New York State Thruway Authority Department of Planning and Policy Development, 1994.

Greene, Francis Vinton. "The Inception of the Barge Canal Project." Buffalo Historical Society Publications. Vol. 13 (1909).

Greene, Frederick S. and Thomas F. Farrell. *The New York State Canal System*. Albany: New York State Public Works Building, n.d.

Kimball, Francis P. *New York—The Canal State; The Story of America's Great Water Route from the Lakes to the Sea, Builder of East and West; with a Discussion of the St. Lawrence Treaty*. Albany: The Argus Press, 1937.

Lock Operator's Log Book. Champlain Barge Canal Lock 5, 1933, 1956.

New York State Barge Canal Plans. Albany: State Engineer and Surveyor [Frank M. Williams]. Supplement to Annual Report, 1920.

New York State Canal Recreation Development Program. Albany: New York State Department of Transportation, Office of Parks and Recreation, 1975.

New York State Department of Transportation Card File with details of state canal boats. Albany: New York State Archives.

"New York State Canal System Monthly Traffic Report 1995 Navigation Season." Albany: New York State Thruway Authority, 1995.

New York Waterways. March-April 1962.

"Oil Shipments on the New York State Canals." New York State Radio Bureau, 17 October 1948.

O'Malley, Charles T. *Low Bridges and High Water on the New York State Barge Canal*. Ellenton, FL: Diamond Mohawk Publishing, 1991.

"The Oswego Canal Field Trip Guide, 14 October 1989." Syracuse: Canal Society of New York State, 1989.

"Oswego Grain Elevator Educational Display." H. Lee White Maritime Museum. Oswego.

"Oswego River Canalling!" [sic] Oswego: Oswego County Department of Promotion and Tourism, 1995.

Press and Sun Bulletin. (New York). 31 March 1997.

Prindle, Tom. "The Tugboat Urger: Ancient Mariner of the Barge Canal." *Sea History*, Summer 1991.

Rome Daily Sentinel (New York). 1903; 2 December 1936; 3 December 1936; 4 December 1936; December 1958.

Salmon, Joseph H. *Economic Survey of the New York State Barge Canal*. n.p.: Economic Survey Committee for New York State Waterways, 1951.

Scothon, Earl. Scrapbook of articles about the New York State Barge Canal. Albany: New York State Museum.

Snider, Clare J., and Michael W. R. Davis. *The Ford Fleet (1923–1989)*. Cleveland, OH: Freshwater Press, 1994.

"State of New York Report of the Joint Legislative Committee on the Barge Canal." Legislative Document Number 36. 1961.

Syracuse Herald. (New York). 2 December 1936; 12 July 1959.

Syracuse Journal (New York). 8 December 1936.

"Tonnage on New York State Canals 1977–1993." Albany: New York State Canal Corporation, n.d.

"Tonnage on New York State Canals, 1900–[1979]." Albany: New York State Department of Transportation, 1968.

"Vessel Registration Forms." Series 17694. Albany: New York State Archives.

Whitford, Noble E. *History of The Barge Canal of New York State*. Albany: J. B. Lyon Company, Printers, 1922.

Williams, Frank M. *Book of Plans New York State Barge Canal*. Issued as a supplement to the Annual Report of the Department of the State Engineer and Surveyor, 1920.

Wilner, M. M. "The New York State Press in the Campaign for Enlargement of the Canals." Buffalo Historical Society Publications. Vol. 13 (1909).

"Workingmen Attention." Penciled manuscript found in copy of the 1901 Bond Report.

Personal interviews

All interviews by the author unless otherwise noted.

Clifford, Bill. 9 June 1994, Barge Canal Inspection Tour.

Costello, Nelson. Interview by Craig Williams, 23 January 1997, Ticonderoga.

Dixie, Desmond. 6 December 1996, Three Rivers Point.

Dwyer, Chuck. Interview by Craig Williams, March 1994.

Fishette, Dennis. 6 June 1995, Barge Canal Inspection Tour.

Folger, Ralph. 28 September 1996, Rensselaer.

Geist, Dan. 27 September 1996, Albany.

Godfrey, Fred. 28 September 1996, Rensselaer.

Granley, Dennis. 6 December 1996, Three Rivers Point.

Hills, Bill. 6 June 1995, Barge Canal Inspection Tour.

Huftill, Austin. Interview by Craig Williams, 8 February 1994.

Jermano, John. 9 June 1994 and 6 June 1995, Barge Canal Inspection Tour.

Mosso, Joseph. 28 September 1996, Rensselaer.

O'Connor, Larry. 11 October 1995, Barge Canal Inspection Tour.

Orzell, Bill, and Sue Orzell. 8 August 1996, DeRuyter.

Peckinpaugh crew. Video interview by Craig Williams, September 1994, Oneida Lake.

Pendergrass, Calvin. Interview by Craig Williams, 6 November 1977, Little Falls.

Pittsley, Bill. 18 January 1996, Brewerton (Lock 23).

Stelatto, Joe. Interview by Craig Williams, 16 January 1997, Loudonville.

Wiles, Dan. 31 March 1997, (telephone).

Wilkins, Evamay. 28 September 1996, Rensselaer.

Wilkins, Evamay. Interview by Craig Williams, 20 May 1993; 25 May 1993; 25 June 1993; 27 July 1993, Waterford.

Index

Bold type indicates an illustration

Other New York State canal books published by Purple Mountain Press

New York State Canals: A Short History
by F. Daniel Larkin

New York's Erie Canal has long been heralded in story and song and the legendary waterway is well known to people throughout the world. Far fewer are aware of the vast, 524-mile canal network that still exists in the state. Although canals in New York first appeared in the eighteenth century, it was the building of the Erie Canal during the first quarter of the nineteenth century that launched New York State and the nation into the canal era; arguably, no other enterprise was as responsible for creating the "Empire State" as was the Erie. There is no question that the Erie Canal was an economic success. In addition to the business it brought the state, more than $120 million in tolls were collected on it during the nineteenth century, paying for its original cost and the first enlargement, as well as maintenance. But many of the state's other canals did not share the Erie's triumph, and the story of New York's canals is one of contrast between those that contributed to the growth and development of the state and those that did not. This accessible history is the first treatment of all of the state's canals in more than 90 years.

Daniel Larkin is a SUNY Oneonta professor and the author of *Pioneer American Railroads: The Mohawk and Hudson & The Saratoga and Schenectady*, published by Purple Mountain Press, and a biography of the engineering genius John B. Jervis.

From the Coalfields to the Hudson: A History of the Delaware & Hudson Canal
by Larry Lowenthal

One hundred years ago the last load of anthracite coal moved down the Delaware & Hudson gravity railway and canal from the coalfields of the Lackawanna Valley to Rondout on the Hudson. This anniversary calls for a new look at this remarkable enterprise. The system that had become hopelessly obsolete by the 1890s—a muddy ditch and an antiquated railway—was the work of one of America's pioneer enterprises. The D&H had to operate a complex business in a hostile environment and, with few examples to guide it, invent itself in the process. Out of necessity the D&H formed a model for modern corporations through its history of almost continual insecurity, upheaval, and controversy. *From the Coalfields to the Hudson* will appeal not only to those interested in the canal but also to fans of the Delaware & Hudson Railroad and students of corporate enterprise in America.

Larry Lowenthal is a historian with the National Park Service and the author of *The Lackawanna Railroad in Northwest New Jersey*.

◆ ◆ ◆

Purple Mountain Press is a publishing company committed to producing the best original books about New York State as well as bringing back into print significant older works of regional interest. For a free catalog, write Purple Mountain Press, Ltd., P.O. Box E3, Fleischmanns, NY 12430; or call 914-254-4062; or fax 914-254-4476; or e-mail Purple@catskill.net. Website: www.catskill.net/purple